Positive HOLINESS

BY **Ken Abraham**

Don't Bite the Apple 'Til You Check for Worms
Designer Genes
Hot Trax (Devotions for Girls)
Hot Trax (Devotions for Guys)
Positive Holiness

For information regarding
speaking engagements and seminars,
please write:

Ken Abraham
P.O. Box 218
Clymer, PA 15728

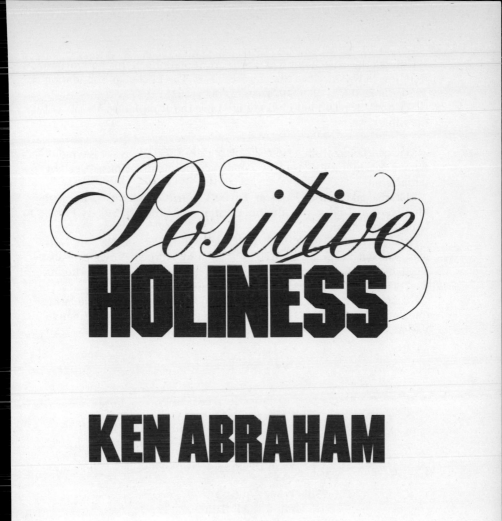

Positive HOLINESS

KEN ABRAHAM

Fleming H. Revell
Old Tappan, New Jersey

Library of Congress Cataloging-in-Publication Data

Abraham, Ken.
Positive holiness / Ken Abraham.
p.   cm.
ISBN 0-8007-1604-3
1. Holiness. I. Title.
BT767.A27 1988
234'.8--dc 19   88-14086
CIP

Copyright © 1988 by Ken Abraham
Published by the Fleming H. Revell Company
Old Tappan, New Jersey 07675
Printed in the United States of America

TO

Dr. Dennis F. Kinlaw, president of Asbury College, Wilmore, Kentucky.

Much of what I have learned and experienced of positive holiness is directly attributable to Dr. Kinlaw's consistent example. Thanks, Doctor, for practicing what you preach! May your ministry be multiplied through these pages.

*   *   *   *   *   *

Also, special thanks to Michael and Doreen Briggs of Birmingham, Michigan. Without Mike's gentle and loving encouragement, *Positive Holiness* might still be a concept stirring in my soul. Because of that special "Briggs' touch," this book will, I hope, be a blessing to many.

Contents

1. Hope for Tomorrow — 9
2. Some Things Don't Mix — 20
3. How Clean Is Clean? — 33
4. What Positive Holiness Is Not — 49
5. How Deep Is Your Love? — 66
6. Overcoming Spiritual Impotence — 78
7. Crimes of the Heart — 93
8. Beauty and the Beast — 112
9. Incentives to Holiness — 135
10. From Here to Eternity — 152
11. Charting Your Course — 165
12. Dead Men Have No Rights — 185
13. More Power to You — 196
14. How Can You Be Holy? — 212

Source Notes — 223

1

Hope for Tomorrow

The flickering candle cast an eerie shadow across the face of the stone walls of the small cubicle where the aged Apostle Peter and his companion, Silas, had been holed up for weeks. Silas sat at a makeshift desk, idly smoothing the parchment upon which he was writing, patiently and silently waiting for Peter to continue his dictation of a letter to the new Christians in Pontus, Galatia, and several other areas of Asia.

Peter seemed almost obsessed with the importance of this letter, as he paced back and forth across the dirt floor of the hideaway.

"I've got to warn them," his quiet but animated voice slit the silence. Silas raised his pen, ready to record the patriarch's words, then put it back in its holder when he realized that Peter was merely thinking aloud.

"They have started out well," Peter said, more to himself than to Silas. "But those new believers need to understand that it is not going to be easy to follow the Christ. They need to know what is coming. They must prepare their hearts and minds, stiffen their wills, and get ready to stand against the impending persecution. . . ." The preacher's voice trailed off, as he became quiet and contemplative once again.

Peter had never actually viewed himself as a prophet, at least, not in the predictive sense. But he could intuitively feel what was happening in the streets of Rome. One did not have to be a visionary to see where current events were leading.

The animosity toward Christians was beginning to surface, spurred on by the Emperor of Rome, the neurotic Nero, whose attitude had recently changed from one of ambivalence to open hostility. When the early believers refused to acknowledge Caesar Nero as Lord, it incensed the already insane despot. Soon, public opinion forced the fledgling group of Roman Christians underground, as the local pendulum began to swing from popularity to persecution. Rumors were rampant that Nero was using Christians as human torches to light up his garden parties and Peter knew that widespread suffering and death were certain to follow. Rome set the standards, and what Rome did, the Empire mirrored.

Peter had seen it all before—back in the early days, when the movement that some had called The Way had taken Jerusalem by storm. At first, the Christians were considered heroes. They had dared to stand against both Rome and Herod. Their message of resurrected life in Christ was appealing and contagious. But the spiritual euphoria of Pentecost quickly dissipated when the fickle crowds suc-

cumbed to the influence of the Jewish scribes and Pharisees. Herod, the cruel and calculating puppet king, was
only too pleased to launch a public persecution of the early
Church. He had one of Peter's closest associates, James, the
brother of John, put to death with the sword. When Herod
saw that it pleased the Jews, he proceeded to arrest and to
imprison Peter as well (Acts 12:1–4).

Only a miraculous deliverance saved Peter from the
same fate that befell James. Freed by an angel in the night,
Peter reported first to the other believers who were gathered at Mary's house. From that point on, Peter operated
much more cautiously and covertly, appearing publicly in
Jerusalem only one more time, at the first major council of
the Church (Acts 15). A few years later, he made his way
to Rome.

Now, as the Apostle pondered the persecutions to
come, one thought loomed largely in his mind: How
could he best prepare the new Christians of Asia for the
difficult days ahead without discouraging them and causing them to despair? Peter chose to be perfectly honest.
Troublesome times were certainly coming, but these
Christians could trust Christ as their present hope and as
their ultimate glory. No matter what their circumstances,
there could be no compromise. God expected better of
them. God demanded better of them.

"Write it, Silas! Write it down and send it with the first
message-bearer you can find:

> . . . Gird your minds for action, keep sober in spirit, fix
> your hope completely on the grace to be brought to you at
> the revelation of Jesus Christ. As obedient children, do
> not be conformed to the former lusts which were yours in
> your ignorance, but like the Holy One who called you, be

*holy yourselves also in all your behavior; because it is
written, "You shall be holy, for I am holy."*

1 Peter 1:13–16

It was not easy to be a Christian in those days. It still
isn't today. It seems that the only people who talk about
how simple (or sissified) it is to serve Christ are the ones
who have never seriously attempted to do so!

On the other hand, many people trumpet statements
like: "God loves you just the way you are! Just believe in
Jesus and that's all that matters!" Such bombastic and
ambiguous generalizations are aberrations of biblical
principles. They are half-truths, at best. Yes, the Bible
says that "God demonstrates His own love toward us, in
that while we were yet sinners, Christ died for us"
(Romans 5:8), but that love should motivate us toward
holiness, because the Bible also emphatically declares
that God hates sin. He cannot tolerate it and He will not
allow you to remain sinful and retain a relationship with
Him at the same time.

In his captivating book, *The Pursuit of Holiness*, Jerry
Bridges accurately points out that:

God hates sin wherever He finds it, in saint and sinner
alike. He does not hate sin in one person and overlook it
in another. . . . In fact, biblical evidence indicates that
God may judge the sins of His saints more severely than
those of the world. David was a man after God's own heart
(Acts 13:22), yet after his sin against Uriah, he was told,
"Now therefore, the sword shall never depart from your
house" (2 Samuel 12:10). Moses, for one act of unbelief,
was excluded from the land of Canaan despite many years
of faithful service. Jonah, for his disobedience, was cast
into a horrible prison in the stomach of a giant fish for

three days and nights, that he might learn not to run from
the command of God.[1]

God has high expectations of you. He says "Be holy . . .
in all your behavior." Why? Because, He says, "You shall
be holy, for I am holy" (1 Peter 1:15, 16).

Holy is the ultimate word for who God is, what His
character is, and what He wants for and from His people.
Some form of the word is used more than eleven hundred
times in the Bible! In the Old Testament, various forms of
the Hebrew word, qds, pronounced "qadosh," occur 830
times; in the New Testament, the Greek word hagios, or
one of its derivations, is used 320 times. Clearly, God is
not leaving it to the imagination who He is, what He is,
and what He expects.

Most people don't know how to deal with this sort of
God because they don't understand this aspect of His
nature. Many people think of God as sort of a genial
"Grandfather in the Sky." They think He sits in His
heavenly rocking chair and smiles knowingly when we
sin or otherwise disappoint Him by failing to live up to
His expectations.

The Bible, however, never gives the impression that
God glosses over sin. Throughout the Holy Scriptures,
God's hatred of sin is contrasted with His absolute
holiness.

Because most people are confused about God's character, they have even less comprehension of what it means
to be a holy man or woman, and what the conduct and
attitudes of a holy person are to be. "Holy?" they ask.
"What does it mean to be holy?"

Many have the misconception that a holy man is
someone similar to an Eastern religious guru, a strange
ascetic who sits cross-legged on the floor, chanting unin-

telligible mumbo jumbo. In recent years, more confusion and suspicion have arisen over cult leaders such as Rajneesh (Bhagwan), whose penchant for "holiness" was reflected in his fleet of over thirty Rolls Royce automobiles.

Others, when they think of a holy man, conjure up images akin to the Ayatollah Khomeini, the irascible ruler of Iran, whose followers toppled the Shah of Iran from power and have been a pain in the Persian Gulf ever since. Understandably, those who regard holiness in this respect see it as an anachronistic, reactionary attempt to control society through insanity, inanity, and the promise of instant paradise for those foolish enough to pledge their allegiance unto death.

Still others assume that a holy man or woman spends the night sleeping on a bed of spikes and wastes away the daylight hours attempting to walk across beds of red hot coals. Not surprisingly, these caricatures of true holiness are not considered to be men and women of good humor or pleasant personality.

Will the Real Holy Person Please Stand Up?

What, then, does it mean to be holy? Close study of Scripture reveals at least three meanings of the word holy. These meanings are not separate, independent definitions, but rather they are three complementary aspects of holiness that seem to go together wherever the word is applied, whether to God, to His people, or to things.

First, a *radiant brightness* is often associated with that which is holy. This can be seen most obviously in the Old Testament, where God is often revealed by fire. An example would be the time God spoke to Moses from the burning bush:

> And the angel of the Lord appeared to him in a blazing fire from the midst of a bush; and he looked, and behold, the bush was burning with fire, yet the bush was not consumed. So Moses said, "I must turn aside now, and see this marvelous sight, why the bush is not burned up." When the Lord saw that he turned aside to look, God called to him from the midst of the bush, and said, "Moses, Moses!" And he said, "Here I am." Then He said, "Do not come near here; remove your sandals from your feet, for the place on which you are standing is holy ground."

> Exodus 3:2–5

Throughout the Old Testament, holiness is linked with brilliant light. You can sense this same radiance in the New Testament, most notably, perhaps, in the Apostle John's descriptive vision of Jesus' appearance in heaven. Trying to convey this overwhelming sight, John writes:

> And in the middle of the lampstands one like a son of man, clothed in a robe reaching to the feet, and girded across His breast with a golden girdle. And His head and His hair were white like white wool, like snow; and His eyes were like a flame of fire; and His feet were like burnished bronze, when it has been caused to glow in a furnace, and His voice was like the sound of many waters. And in His right hand He held seven stars; and out of His mouth came a sharp two-edged sword; and His face was like the sun shining in its strength.

> Revelation 1:13–16

Scholars often disagree as to how much of John's vision should be taken literally and how much of it is symbolic. However you interpret it, the full impact was not lost upon John. His response was probably what yours would be in similar circumstances. John said: "And when I saw Him, I fell at His feet as a dead man" (Revelation 1:17).

When a man or woman comes into intimate contact with the Holy God, radiance is the result. Moses only beheld God's glory from behind, but he was so profoundly affected that his brother Aaron and the people of Israel were afraid to come near him (Exodus 34:29, 30). Although Moses was not even aware of the change in his external appearance, apparently his face simply radiated with the glow of God upon it.

Something similar still happens today when a person spends time in the presence of God. Perhaps you have seen other Christian people who seem to glow. Their eyes have an unusual sparkle; their mouths tend to turn quickly into smiles. They seem to have a special lilt to their walk. Their countenances radiate warmth and joy. Their lives seem to virtually overflow with the love of Christ.

You say, "They've got something I don't have!"

No. They don't have *something*. Something has *them*. Better still, Someone has them. These radiant individuals have surrendered the control of their lives to Jesus Christ. They have allowed Him to cleanse their hearts and to fill them with His Holy Spirit, and they are now living in holiness on a day-by-day basis.

This is what I call "positive holiness." It is not comprised of rules and regulations; it is love and joy, peace and power; it is the perpetual infilling and overflowing of the supernatural Holy Spirit in and through the life of an ordinary believer.

Positive holiness is attractive; it is inviting; it is contagious! Furthermore, it is a natural result of having Jesus Christ dwelling within you. It is genuine; you can't fake it. Neither is it possible to conjure up true holiness. You don't get out of bed, take a shower, brush your teeth, put on your clothes, and then dab on a dash of radiant brightness before you go out the door. Positive holiness is the real thing and cheap imitations can't compete with it.

Samuel Logan Brengle, who was the Salvation Army's best-known holiness teacher, was a shining example of positive holiness. Holiness to Brengle meant a "be-happy attitude," regardless of the situation. Those who knew him said that, despite a rigorous travel schedule punctuated by severe physical sickness and awful emotional stress, Sam Brengle always seemed to have a twinkle in his eye and a radiance about his facial appearance.

Once Brengle visited a family in order to make a pastoral call, only to discover that the father was not at home. He chatted briefly with the mother and children, prayed with them, and then went on his way.

Later that night, when the father arrived home from work, his little boy met him at the door. "Daddy, Daddy," the small child shrieked excitedly. "You should have been here today! Daddy, Jesus has been here!"

Is that what your friends say after spending time with you?

In his classic work, *Holiness*, the nineteenth-century expositor, Bishop J. C. Ryle wrote straightforwardly:

> Sanctification [i.e., holiness], again, is *a thing that will always be seen*. Like the Great Head of the Church, from whom it springs, it "cannot be hid." "Every tree is known by his own fruit" (Luke 6:44). A truly sanctified person may be so clothed with humility that he can see in

himself nothing but infirmity and defects. . . . Like the
righteous, in the mighty parable of the sheep and the
goats, he may not see that he has done anything worthy of
his Master's notice and commendation. . . . But whether
he sees it himself or not, others will always see in him a
tone, and taste, and character, and habit of life unlike that
of other men. The very idea of a man being "sanctified,"
while no holiness can be seen in his life, is flat nonsense
and a misuse of words. . . . A "saint" in whom nothing
can be seen but worldliness or sin, is a kind of monster not
recognized in the Bible![2]

Holiness often shows up first in a person's face. In one
town where Brengle was preaching, a deaf woman sat on
the front row throughout the service. As Brengle invited
his listeners to meet Christ, the woman shocked the
congregation by being the first person to respond. She
stepped to the front of the room, knelt down, and began to
sob softly.

The woman's daughter, seated near the rear of the
sanctuary, saw her mother's response and hurried to join
the elderly woman on her knees. Thinking that her
mother had been healed, the daughter knelt beside her
and asked aloud, "Mother, could you hear the sermon?"

When she realized that her mother was still deaf, she
repeated her question more slowly, allowing time for the
sobbing woman to read her lips, "Mother, could you hear
the sermon?"

"No," the older woman answered. "I didn't hear anything, but I saw Jesus in that man's face."

What a positive witness! A holy person possesses a
quality that speaks more loudly than words; he or she
radiates a genuine exuberance, a brightness that both
believers and unbelievers find attractive.

I was the speaker for a series of services at a beautiful

Baptist church in northern Georgia when I received what I thought was one of the finest compliments of my life. A sophisticated, well-dressed woman gushed in her deep Georgian drawl, "Ken, you just seem to glow!"

I thanked her profusely and assured her that it was Christ in me who was shining through to her.

The next week, I was speaking at a youth retreat in the small community of Middletown, Pennsylvania, where I thought I would extend the same compliment to an effervescent group of counselors. "You just seem to glow," I told them. Unfortunately, I had forgotten that Middletown is the location of America's most infamous nuclear accident, at Three Mile Island.

Radioactivity notwithstanding, there is a radiant brightness about a holy life. Of course, the opposite is true, too. Apart from Christ's indwelling your life, you are condemned to darkness. The Bible tells us, "God is light, and in Him there is no darkness at all" (1 John 1:5). If you choose to refuse His light, the darkness will envelop you.

A friend of mine provided great insight into this truth. He said, "I was walking along the beach one evening, just before sunset, when I noticed a curious phenomenon. I discovered that as I walked with my face toward the sun, I could enjoy its warmth and light, but when I turned my back on the sun, I'd have to walk in my own shadow."

The same principle is true spiritually. If you turn your back on the Son, you will be forced to walk in the shadow created by your own life. On the other hand, when you walk with your face toward the Son, you will enjoy His warmth, light, and glory—and there will be a radiant brightness about your life.

Some Things Don't Mix

Okay, I confess. I love my coffee. If you are a fellow caffeine fiend, stop reading right now. Put this book down and go pour yourself a fresh cupful of the delicious liquid. Even if you are a decaffeinated coffee nut (token members of all true coffee klatches), please take advantage of this opportunity to satisfy your desires. Go ahead; I'll wait for you. Only a "java junkie" will genuinely appreciate the story I am about to tell you.

If you happen to be one of those extremely strange human beings who gets nauseous at even the *smell* of perking coffee, please pause for a moment of prayer on behalf of those of us who are half-crazed caffeine consumers. While you're doing that, stay here and hold this page. I'll be right back. I'm going out for a cup of coffee!

Okay, are you ready? Be careful not to spill anything on these pages. This book is valuable, you know.

It happened one of those mornings when I just did not want to get out of bed. I had worked late for several nights in a row, with little sleep in between. Now the clock's incessant buzzing simply would not quit. *Whoever invented "snooze controls" should be shot,* I thought to myself as I rolled onto my side, burying my ear in the pillow while simultaneously pulling the blankets up over my head to dull the sound in my other ear.

My wife, Angela, discerned my dilemma and mercifully reached over to the clock and silenced the snooze mechanism. She crawled slowly out of bed, tiptoed to the kitchen, and put on a pot of coffee.

"Ken," she called softly, "time to get up. I'm going to shower before breakfast, but the coffee is on."

I groggily poked my head out from beneath the covers and sniffed. Already, the aroma had wafted from room to room, permeating the air of our apartment. That was all the encouragement I needed. I rolled out of bed, threw on a robe, and staggered toward the kitchen, following the smell of freshly brewed coffee.

When I arrived in the kitchen, I heard the familiar sound of our microwave oven whirring in the corner. "What a wonderful woman that Angela is!" I thought out loud. "She not only put on a pot of fresh-brewed coffee, but she is warming a cup of instant coffee in the microwave for me." I peered through the glass oven door, and, sure enough, there it was, a rich, dark cup of my favorite fluid.

The microwave buzzer sounded, signaling the readiness of a faithful friend. I quickly removed the cup from the oven and poured in some cream. *Hmm-mmm, this is going to be good!* I thought as I anxiously took a huge gulp, without even stirring the contents. I had swallowed the whole mouthful before the taste registered on my tongue.

"*Yeeyech!*" I roared. "This isn't coffee! This stuff is *prune juice!*" I looked more closely at the contents of the cup, and even in the dark kitchen I could see that the cream had already separated from the hot brown juice, causing the cream to curdle and rise to the top of the container in yellow-white globules. I could just imagine the same thing happening in my stomach. "Blaahh!" I bellowed. "Angela, watch out; here I come!" I yelled as I bounded toward the bathroom.

Some things just don't mix. Such as prune juice and cream. And oil and water. Unrighteousness and righteousness. The profane and the holy. Some things were intended to be perpetually separated.

The concept of separation is the second of the three fundamental meanings of holiness. Negatively, men and women are to be separated *from* the secular world's sinful actions and attitudes. Positively, holy men and women are to be separated *to* God. You and I are to be set apart and removed from the common, profane things of this world, while we are set apart, or consecrated, to God for His special use and for His glory. Positive holiness means that we belong to God. We are positively destined for and devoted to the service of our Lord God.

We see a graphic picture of how this separation impacts upon our lives, both negatively and positively, in Paul's second letter to the Corinthians. He exhorted them to be separate from the nonbelievers in the world, while at the same time he reminded them of the positive promise of God's personal, paternal care.

Do not be bound together with unbelievers; for what partnership have righteousness and lawlessness, or what fellowship has light with darkness? Or what harmony has Christ with Belial, or what has a believer in common with an unbeliever? Or what agreement has the temple of God with idols? For we are the temple of the living God; just as God said, "I will dwell in them and walk among them; And I will be their God, and they shall be My people. Therefore, come out from their midst and be separate," says the Lord. "And do not touch what is unclean; And I will welcome you. And I will be a father to you, And you shall be sons and daughters to Me," Says the Lord Almighty.

2 Corinthians 6:14–18

Because of the emphasis in this passage upon separation from the secular world, many Christians have assumed the notion that God wants them to be *weird*. "Let's get weird for Jesus!" seems to be their motto. They falsely figure that the "weirder" they live, the holier they are.

"Don't you know that God wants a *peculiar* people?" they puff piously.

Peculiar perhaps; weird and wacky, never. Granted, God does require His people to be different from the world, but nowhere in Scripture does He command you to be a dolt. If you are weird, please don't blame God; you were probably pretty strange before you met Him! God doesn't make normal people into weirdos; He takes weirdos and transforms them into normal, healthy, whole people.

There is a sense, however, in which separation is negative. The form of the Hebrew word for holiness that implies this most often is *kodesh,* from *qadosh*. It has the meaning of "being cut off," or separated. When this word is used in reference to God, it designates that God is set apart from His creation. He is not a part of this world; He is above it, beyond it. He is unique. No other god can compare with Him.

Early in their existence as a holy, called-out, chosen people, the Israelites realized this truth. Even before the Law was given at Sinai, the Hebrews witnessed God's awesome, holy power. One unforgettable example, indelibly impressed upon the memory of Israel, was their miraculous deliverance from Pharaoh. Moses and the people of God crossed through the Red Sea on dry land and then watched in amazement while Pharaoh's army was inundated by that same body of water. The Scripture says, "When Israel saw the great power which the Lord had used against the Egyptians, the people feared the Lord, and they believed in the Lord and in His servant Moses" (Exodus 14:31). The people were awestruck by the supernatural power of their holy God. None of the Egyptian gods had that sort of awful power. Consequently, the Hebrews began to sing:

> Who is like Thee among the gods, O Lord?
> Who is like Thee, majestic in holiness,
> Awesome in praises, working wonders?
>
> Exodus 15:11

God was thought to be unapproachable because of His stupendous, dangerous, frightful power. The idea was, "Don't mess with a God like that! He is not like us. He is different; He is 'awfully other' than we are." Granted, God was also thought to be magnificent and unapproachable because of His moral and ethical excellence, as well as His sheer majesty, but the sense of fear that His "otherness" evoked should not be underestimated.

Because of this, Rudolf Otto, a mystical early-twentieth-century German scholar, coined an interesting phrase to describe "the holy," and in particular, the "otherness" of God. Otto called it the "mysterium tremendum," or the "awful mystery." Otto was troubled by the fact that although God's separateness is a cause of great fear, man continues to hold an eerie fascination with Him and desires a relationship with Him. Echoing Otto, R. C. Sproul says, "Nothing is more dreadful to man, more terrifying to the mind, than to be brought within the holy. Here we begin to tremble as we are brought into the presence of the *mysterium tremendum*."

Certainly, there is mystery concerning this aspect of God's character, and yes, it ought to scare the wits out of any thinking person when he or she imagines coming into the presence of such an awesome God. Nevertheless, just because God is separate from His creation does not mean that He is unknowable, impersonal, or uninvolved. On the contrary, His repeated invitation to Israel and to us has always been "come out of their midst and be separate . . . And I will welcome you. And I will be a father to you, And you shall be sons and daughters to Me" (2 Corinthians 6:17, 18).

God wants to enter into an intimate relationship with you, but it will only be on His terms. He says, "You shall be holy, for I am holy" (1 Peter 1:16). Is God being a bully or an obstinate brat who says, "If you won't play My way, I'm going to take My ball and go home"? No. Remember, it is not only God's ball; it is His game and His ball field! If you want a relationship with Him, you must be ready to play by His rules, to separate yourself from any uncleanness, and to allow Him to make you holy.

Understand first that it is only because God is holy that you have any hope of ever being holy. Any holiness you experience is what theologians refer to as "derived" holiness. It comes from God alone, and its only source is in Him. You are not intrinsically holy. (You didn't *really* need me to tell you that, did you?) Furthermore, you do not become holy because of your good looks, pleasant personality, religious efforts, or indefatigable self-improvement programs. You don't necessarily become holy by going to church, reading your Bible, or even fasting and praying, as admirable as those activities may be.

True holiness comes only from God. Only He is holy in and of Himself, and as such, only He can impart His holiness to any thing, place, or person. When He does so, He sets apart that portion of His creation and it *becomes* holy.

The Separation of Things

Oftentimes in the Old Testament, things were set apart by God or for God's use and were therefore declared *holy*. You may be surprised to discover the number of ordinary objects that came to be considered extraordinary simply because they were removed from common use, cleansed, and set apart as special unto God. Certain pots and pans were declared holy. Specific people and places were designated as holy. The Tabernacle and later the Temple were called holy. Certain times and dates were set apart as being holy unto God. The Sabbath *day* was said to be holy.

The Bible also speaks of holy assemblies or convocations (Exodus 12:16), "holy garments" (Exodus 28:2), "holy anointing oil" (Exodus 37:29), "the holy city" (Matthew 4:5), "holy Scriptures" (Romans 1:2), "holy apostles" (Ephesians 3:5), "a holy kiss" (1 Corinthians 16:20), "a holy calling" (2 Timothy 1:9), "holy brethren" (Hebrews 3:1), "a holy priesthood" (1 Peter 2:5), "a holy nation" (1 Peter 2:9), and a host of other *things* that were hailed as holy for no other reason except that they were set apart for God's honor.

Nowhere in Scripture is it recorded that God sanctified

something without reason or purpose. When pots and pans were set apart, they were to be used for His glory. It was their service to the Lord that made them holy. They were not considered holy because of their size, shape, decoration, or design. In fact, prior to being set apart, they were considered ordinary utensils.

Similarly, Solomon's lavish Temple built in Jerusalem *became* holy when the glory of God filled it (2 Chronicles 7:1–4). Until that time, it was just a building, an immense edifice that would have otherwise been used to stroke Solomon's ego of approximately the same size. Of course, nobody really believed that God could be contained in a house made by human hands. Solomon himself, in his prayer of dedication at the Temple's inauguration, declared "But will God indeed dwell on the earth? Behold, heaven and the highest heaven cannot contain Thee, how much less this house which I have built!" (1 Kings 8:27.) Still, the Temple was a place set apart to facilitate the worship of God. That was the paramount purpose for its existence.

In the same fashion, God set apart the seventh day of the week as a *Sabbath day* (Exodus 20:8–11). The Sabbath did not have thirty-six hours instead of twenty-four; nor did the sun necessarily shine more brightly on the Sabbath than on the other six days of the week. It was just another day, except that it was set apart as a day of worship to God—and that made it holy.

The Separation of People

Obviously, if inanimate objects can be set apart, and if days and dates can be dedicated completely to God, then it is a small step to believe that human beings can be set apart for His glory, too. Yes, you can be made holy! But there is a major difference that takes place when a man or woman is set apart for God's glory—the Lord fills that person with His supernatural Holy Spirit! God does not fill pots and pans with Himself. He doesn't indwell days or buildings. His Spirit does not pervade plans and promotions, methods or machinery. Yet the Lord fills *men* and *women* with Himself, sets them apart for special service, then works through their personalities to perform His will and His wonders.

Human beings who are holy do, however, share many of the spiritual characteristics that are ascribed to any *thing* that is holy. They, too, reflect a radiant brightness. They, too, are set apart. Furthermore, they are not set apart by accident or without purpose. God does not say, "Okay, gang. Now you are holy. Now you are free to go out and do your own thing." The exact opposite is true. If a man or woman is made holy, it is for a purpose. History is filled with examples of ordinary men and women who accomplished extraordinary achievements for God because they were set apart for special service in His Kingdom. Natural men and women were given supernatural abilities to do both the miraculous and the mundane tasks, that the Name of Jesus might be magnified.

Few men and women in history have lived out this truth any more dramatically than William and Catherine Booth, founders of the Salvation Army. At the age of thirteen, William yielded his heart to God and committed himself, as much as he knew how, to the service of Christ. Shortly thereafter, when young Booth heard the dynamic preaching of American evangelist James Caughey, a desire was kindled within William's heart to win men and women to Jesus. But what could a teenager do?

After a long time of prayer and reading the Bible, he hit upon an idea. *I'll simply read the Scriptures to them!* he thought. But Booth was not content to merely read his Bible in the comfort and safety of his parents' home. No, God was training this young man for his future ministry.

William took his Bible and went out to the main thoroughfares of Nottingham, England. There, he stood on a busy street corner and read the Scriptures aloud to any passersby who would take time to listen. Sometimes, when William felt exceptionally brave, he even ventured to deliver some extemporaneous remarks concerning the passage he was reading.

The results were much as one might expect. William was mocked, ridiculed, jeered at, and humiliated by the local gentry of Nottingham. His reading and commentary so infuriated other members of the community that on more than one occasion, bricks were hurled at young Booth in an attempt to silence him. Still, he persisted undaunted.

At seventeen, against the wishes of his doctor, William Booth became a bona fide preacher of the Gospel. "The doctor advised him that his health was so poor that he was totally unfit for the strain of the life of a . . . minister."[1] History does not record the physician's sentiments when, fifteen years later, the brash Booth began the organization that is now known as the Salvation Army, a ministry famous for its hearty, open-air street meetings. Today, the Army numbers more than 4 million "soldiers" who work for God in over eighty-six countries.

The "mother" of that huge Army was Catherine Mumford Booth, William's wife and constant co-worker. Catherine had been converted at the age of sixteen, but her own entrance into holy living was the pivotal spiritual experience that later launched the Army's extensive emphasis upon holiness of the heart. Describing the struggle that changed her life, Catherine said:

I struggled through the day until a little after six in the evening, when William joined me in prayer. We had a blessed season. While he was saying, "Lord we open our hearts to receive Thee," that word was spoken to my soul: "Behold, I stand at the door and knock. If any man hear my voice, and open unto me, I will come in and sup with him." I felt sure He had been knocking, and oh, how I yearned to receive Him as a perfect Saviour! But oh, the inveterate habit of unbelief! How wonderful that God should have borne so long with me.

When we got up from our knees I lay on the sofa, exhausted with the effort and excitement of the day. William said, "Don't you lay all on the altar?" I replied, "I am sure I do!" Then he said, "And isn't the altar holy?" I replied in the language of the Holy Ghost, "The altar is most holy, and whatsoever toucheth it is holy." Then said he, "Are you not holy?" I replied with my heart full of emotion and with some faith, "Oh, I think I am." Immediately the word was given me to confirm my faith, "Now are ye clean through the word I have spoken unto you." And I took hold—true, with a trembling hand, and not unmolested by the tempter, but I held fast the beginning of my confidence, and it grew stronger, and from that moment I have dared to reckon myself dead indeed unto sin, but alive unto God through Jesus Christ, my Lord.[2]

Catherine Booth knew what it meant to be set apart for God. For this spunky Salvationist, however, separation did not mean isolation. In fact, it was her understanding of holiness that thrust her into active participation in helping to solve the most pernicious problems of society. It was because she was set apart to God that she could not sit idly by without trying to change the evils of the world. In many ways, Mrs. Booth was far ahead of her time in the area of women's equality and social concern. She often

castigated self-centered women for their laziness and lack
of spiritual motivation.

> "It will be a happy day for England," she once observed,
> "when Christian ladies transfer their attention from poo-
> dles and terriers to destitute and starving children." She
> reminded women that living for pleasure, and filling their
> days with eating, drinking, dressing, riding and
> sight-seeing, left no time to serve God. They were too
> occupied with self, she said, to develop spiritual
> resources.[3]

One of the ways Catherine Booth decided that she
could emphasize her separation from the world was
through her clothing. Ironically, she was not content to
wear ordinary garb which afforded only a barely notice-
able, nondescript differentiation between her appearance
and her secular contemporaries. She wanted the difference to be obvious to even a casual observer. As such, in
a day when most intelligent, sophisticated women were
piling on the powder and the petticoats, Catherine de-
signed a new look for the women of the Salvation Army—
a uniform!

Although the uniform might seem plain by today's
standards, it clearly stated to the world that the woman
wearing it was on important business and was worthy of
respect. Catherine's rationale was simple:

> It seemed clear to me from the teaching of the Bible that
> Christ's people should be separate from the world in
> everything which denoted character and that they should
> not only be separate but appear so. Otherwise what benefit
> would their separation confer upon others? As I advanced
> in religious experience I became more and more con-
> vinced that my appearance ought to be such as to show

everybody with whom I came in contact that I have
renounced the pomp and vanities of the world, and that I
belonged to Christ.[4]

Over the years, Catherine's uniform has become a symbol,
not simply of separation unto the Lord, but of holy
concern and involvement in some of society's ugliest
sores and worst wounds. Of course, it is not necessary to
wear a uniform or any other particular style of clothing in
order to be holy, or concerned about the needs of others,
and involved in making a positive difference in a community.

Catherine and William Booth were set apart unto the
Lord; they were "clothed in the Holy Spirit," and their
holy lives resulted in effective and fruitful service for
Christ. The Booths' influence continues to this day
through their writings and through the Salvation Army's
positive impact upon society.

The Tough Question

How about you? Has your life been set apart for God's
glory? Have you allowed the Lord to fill you with His holy
presence and make you a positively holy person? Has He
given you a fresh sense of divine power and purpose in
your life? He will, if you will permit Him to do so. He can
do that and much more!

place at the pool. As he hurriedly attempted to sneak through inspection, the voice of Authority was heard to say, "Jaki, go and wash your hands!"

"But, Miss, I have washed them!"

"Jaki, look at them—they're filthy!"

"Please, Miss, I *did* wash them! I did, I truly did."

"Miss, he did," shouted a friend. "I saw him, down at the pool."

Authority was unimpressed.

"Jaki, just look at your hands. Are they clean?"

"But I washed—I washed. I really washed!" wailed the culprit.

"I merely asked you to *look* at your hands, and tell me if you think they are clean," was the patient rejoinder of Authority.

As Jaki turned to leave the line and make his way back to the water hole, the luckless lad could be heard muttering, "But how clean do my hands have to be to be clean?"[1]

Jaki's question hits the nail right on the head for most of us. *How clean is clean?* Better still, how clean is holy? And how clean do I have to be in order to be holy?

The question is especially relevant because the third related meaning of the word holy is purity. God's holiness is that of radiant brightness, separation, and purity. The Scriptures clearly state that if we are to know intimate communion with Him, we are to possess those same qualities.

The psalmist pondered:

> *Who may ascend into the hill of the Lord?*
> *And who may stand in His holy place?*
> *He who has clean hands and a pure heart,*
> *Who has not lifted up his soul to falsehood,*
> *And has not sworn deceitfully.*

> *Psalms 24:3, 4*

Who is going to see God? In the Beatitudes, Jesus said "Blessed are the pure in heart, for they shall see God" (Matthew 5:8).

Pure in heart? Jesus, are You kidding? Who talks about purity these days? Who even *thinks* about purity in the kind of world in which we live? In a world where smut and perversion scream at us from our televisions and radios, where billboards belch anti-biblical messages, in a world where our moral values are being repeatedly mauled and maligned in the magazines, movies, and music of our culture; in a world filled with moral filth and ethical degradation, who talks about purity? In a public school system where one out of two teenagers has already squandered away his or her virginity, where over 50 percent of the students have experimented with drugs or alcohol, and an overwhelming 75 percent cheat regularly on their tests; in such a world, who talks about purity anymore?

And why shouldn't the kids cheat? They've been trained well by their parents. For years, the children have watched Mom and Dad cheat the salesclerks, cheat in business, cheat the Internal Revenue Service, and often cheat on each other. In a world where cheaters usually win, who talks about purity?

In a world where might makes right, and where nice guys finish last according to Leo Durocher, and where *Nice Guys Sleep Alone* according to Bruce Feirstein—in such a world as ours, who talks about purity anymore?

Who talks about purity?

God does.

His standards do not vacillate with every wind and whim of our society. His commands remain solidly the same. He requires that I be holy, that I be morally blameless, that I be clean, pure, and spotless.

Now, that creates a serious problem: I know me! I mean,

I *know* me; I am painfully aware of my failures and my sins, and I know that if forced to stand alone on my own merit before God, I wouldn't stand a chance of entering heaven. Unfortunately, the percentages would be high and my margin of error would be extremely slight if one calculated the possibility of me hitting hell. Because, basically, apart from Jesus Christ, I am a sinful person.

You probably have the same problem. God says you are to be holy and you are *not* holy. Your dilemma is further complicated because you know that it is absolutely impossible for you ever to *become* holy by your own self-effort. Perhaps you have already tried that route—and failed. You know how it goes: Just when you think your hands are clean and your heart is pure, God shines His searchlight upon you, and the brilliance of His holiness discloses the dirt that you allowed to remain hidden in the shadows of your life.

Disgusting, isn't it?

The Apostle Paul must have experienced something similar. See if you can identify with his sentiments:

> For that which I am doing, I do not understand; for I am not practicing what I would like to do, but I am doing the very thing I hate. . . . for the wishing is present in me, but the doing of the good is not. For the good that I wish, I do not do; but I practice the very evil that I do not wish. But if I am doing the very thing I do not wish, I am no longer the one doing it, but sin which dwells in me.

Romans 7:15, 18–20

Paul saw the issues with stark clarity. He could have said, "I'm supposed to be good, and yet I keep being bad.

God knows I want to be pure, yet for all of my efforts, I remain impure, and there seems to be nothing I can do about it." Instead, he made no attempt to justify himself.

A little boy was constantly getting into trouble. Everywhere he went, trouble seemed to follow him, at home, at school, even at church. His Sunday school teacher, however, was a paragon of virtue and the boy admired her immensely. One day, as he was comparing his conduct to hers, he lamented with despair evident in his voice, "Teacher you're so good and I'm so bad. I just wish you could crawl down inside of me; then, I'd be good like you are!"

Though the youngster's theology leaves much to be desired, he unwittingly struck upon the secret to positive holiness. The key to positive, victorious, Christ-like conduct is "Christ in you, the hope of glory" (Colossians 1:27, italics mine). Nowhere does the Word of God imply that successful Christian living depends upon your abilities, spiritual or otherwise. It is not you at your best attempting to live up to God's holiness. It all depends upon Him. Face it: You can't measure up to His standards. By rights, you deserve to die for what you have said, thought, and done. Furthermore, you cannot take away a single sin that you have ever committed.

But, thank God, Jesus can! Do you remember Paul's pointed question after his despondent description of his defeat in the face of sin? Paul cried out, ". . . Who will set me free from the body of this death?" Then, as though somebody had switched on a light bulb in his heart and mind, he suddenly perceived the answer to his own question: "Thanks be to God through Jesus Christ our Lord!. . ." (Romans 7:24, 25.) Paul saw that Jesus was his only hope of holiness.

Costly Victory

Christ's sacrifice on the cross purchased both our salvation from sin and the ability of living victoriously over sin. His blood paid the total price for our full salvation.

Modern-day believers have been slow to grasp this principle. Most current Christians confess some degree of confusion when discussing the blood of Jesus. They tend to regard "the blood" as an archaic ritual, left over from a less sophisticated society; a needless reminder of our gory past that retains little significance or relevance for today's positive, upbeat, upscale Christianity.

Perhaps part of our perplexity results from such puzzling biblical expressions as "drinking Christ's blood" or "washing our robes in the blood of the Lamb." What does that mean to anyone who was not raised in Sunday school? Even more confusing to many new Christians are some of the lyrics to the songs we sing in church:

"There Is Power in the Blood!"
"Are You Washed in the Blood of the Lamb?"
"What can wash away my sins? Nothing but the blood of Jesus."

For many post-baby-boom disciples of Christ, these songs seem almost absurd, making absolutely no sense at all. What does the blood have to do with high-tech media ministries? Where does the blood fit into our contemporary Christian music? What significance does the blood have in my personal success or in my motivational methods? How does the blood compare to current concepts of Christianity? What difference does the blood of Jesus make when it comes to day-care centers, church directories, budgets, babies, and baptisms? These are valid questions for a generation that Francis Schaeffer often described as having no "Christian memory."

Many modern-day Christians, although devoutly dedicated to Christ, have little comprehension of some of the most basic tenets of their faith. Many have no repository of stored biblical data, inherited from parents or grandparents, upon which they can build. Consequently, we now have a generation or two of believers whose faith is existential; their common testimony is, "This is what Jesus did for me. Here is my experience." One could argue that it is better to have an experience with Christ than to have mere head knowledge of Him. Nevertheless, it is important that we know the foundations upon which we stand.

Therefore, it is vital that we renew our emphasis upon this basic element of our salvation, the blood atonement of Christ. Furthermore, it is imperative that we comprehend the doctrine of the blood of Jesus if we are ever to understand and experience personal holiness. The holiness of God and the Cross of Christ are irreversibly linked together. It is no accident that we find the blood most often mentioned in the Old Testament in the Book of Leviticus, and in the New Testament in the Books of Hebrews and Revelation. In these same books, God repeatedly reminds us of His demand for holiness and purity among His people.

Blood sacrifices were familiar sights in ancient Israel. Thousands of animals were slaughtered in the Jerusalem Temple area every year. The historian, Josephus, estimated that at the time of Jesus Christ, over a quarter of a million lambs were sacrificed during Passover ceremonies alone!

The Old Testament sacrificial system was infused with symbolism; it was a method by which the worshiper could vicariously express his or her devotion to God by substituting the life of an animal for his or her own life. The sacrifice, therefore, could not be just *any* animal. On the contrary, the sacrifice offered to God had to be special. First, it was required to be the personal property of the sacrificer. If a person did not possess a proper animal, he or she could purchase one fit for offering. Second, the animal had to be "perfect," free from defects, without blemish. It had to be the absolute best that the sacrificer could offer to God.

When the worshiper brought his animal to the Lord, it was put upon the altar in such a position that it faced the Holy Place in the Temple. The person making the sacrifice would then place his hands on the head of the offering, while stating the purpose for his or her sacrifice, or confessing his sin. It was as though the sins of the sacrificer were being transferred to the sacrifice. Then, the animal was violently killed, usually by slitting its throat with a sharp knife.

The shed blood was offered to God by a priest. Depending upon the type of sacrifice, the blood was either sprinkled on the altar, thrown against the altar, or poured out at the base of the altar.

Sadly, all of these Old Testament sacrifices could never really take away the power of sin. Although God honored these sacrifices, it was only because they pointed to the ultimate sacrifice, Jesus Christ. It was His blameless life that constituted the perfect sacrifice. When He hung on Calvary's cross, He was being sacrificed for you and for me. He had never sinned. He never said an evil word or did an evil deed. He was dying for those of us who have sinned so horribly. It was His death, the violent nailing of His body to the cross, as He offered himself to God on your behalf and mine, that purchased our salvation. He paid the price for our sins.

Perhaps that is why the prophet Isaiah proclaimed as he peered into the future:

> Surely our griefs He Himself bore,
> And our sorrows He carried. . . .
> He was pierced through for our transgressions,
> He was crushed for our iniquities,
> The chastening for our well-being fell upon Him.
>
> Isaiah 53:4, 5

This substitutionary atonement, the fact that Jesus died in our place, is also prefigured in the Jewish feast of Passover. Passover was a God-ordained time of celebration each year, commemorating the deliverance of the Hebrew people from the bondage of slavery in Egypt. The original Passover climaxed a series of severe plagues inflicted upon Pharaoh and the Egyptian people. In preparation for their deliverance, God instructed His people to slay a lamb, early in the evening, and then use a celerylike bush known as hyssop to sprinkle the blood of the lamb over the doorway of their homes. The people were then to go inside the house and stay there until it was time to go. God had assured them through Moses that no harm would come to the families who were hidden behind the blood.

Once all of the family members were inside, they were to eat a special, symbolic meal together. The flesh of the slain lamb was to be eaten, along with bitter herbs and unleavened bread. The meal was to be eaten quickly, with their sandals on and a staff in their hands. Everything about the meal conveyed a reminder of either the bitterness of their Egyptian bondage or the haste and suddenness of their divine deliverance and departure.

While the obedient Hebrew families observed this holy feast, the angel of God passed over Egypt killing the firstborn child and the firstborn animal of every family who had not prepared by applying the blood of the lamb to the doorway of their homes. Understandably, an awful cry of grief and anguish arose in Egypt that night, for the Bible says, "there was no home where there was not someone dead" (Exodus 12:30).

Immediately, Pharaoh called for Moses and Aaron and commanded them to get out of his country. The two leaders of God's people did not wait for Pharaoh to change his mind, but took prompt action in gathering the people together and leading them out. The Lord delivered His people that night.

As predicted (Exodus 3:22), the sons of Israel did not go out empty-handed, but actually plundered the nation of Egypt as they went (Exodus 12:36). In a way, the Egyptians plundered themselves, by giving the Israelites "going-away presents." The attitude of Pharaoh's plague-ridden people was: "Here, take my silver; take my gold; take my finest clothing; take anything you want; just please leave!"

The Israelites' journey to freedom had begun. They did experience a slight obstacle at the Red Sea, where an obstinate Pharaoh and his army took their last bath. Nevertheless, the real deliverance took place the night of Passover.

Consequently, God instructed the Israelites to institute a yearly feast, similar to that first Passover meal, to remind them of His supernatural deliverance. Every year since, orthodox Jews have done this regardless of where they have been located. In Jesus' time, many of the Jews would return to Jerusalem, if at all possible, to join in a corporate celebration. Passover was always quite a spectacle.

On the afternoon before the Passover meal was to be eaten, thousands of lambs were killed in the Temple area, and the blood of each sacrifice was offered to God on the altar. The blood was caught in a basin and then passed down a line of priests. The priest nearest the altar area took the basin of blood and threw it against the base of the altar. From there, the blood flowed into the drains below the Temple.

Meanwhile, the Temple choirs and the huge throng of worshipers repeatedly sang "The Hallel," the hymns of praise and worship found in Psalms 113–118. Other people responded by shouting "Praise ye the Lord!" or "Hallelujah!" This activity continued all day long.

Picture this spectacle:

- The enormous mass of worshipers
- The bleating of the frightened animals as they waited to be sacrificed
- The incessant flashing of the knife
- The spurting blood
- The priests in their white robes, that quickly became spattered with lambs' blood
- The blood in the basins being passed from priest to priest
- The blood splashing against the altar base
- The fountain of blood pouring over the altar area spilling out onto the marble pavement of the Temple floor
- The reeking smell of blood permeating the air
- All the while, the Temple choirs and the worshiping crowd are singing and chanting their praises to God.

The tragedy of all tragedies took place one Friday afternoon before Passover, a day that, strangely, the world

has since referred to as "Good." On that day, amid the
spiritual spectacle and the mayhem, the masses missed
the true meaning of those millions of sacrifices that had
been offered at the Temple over the years. Because, there
in the distance, just beyond the splendor of the Temple
and outside the gates of the city, rose a lonely, ugly
hilltop known as Golgotha, "the place of the skull"—a
hill called Mount Calvary. On that hill, stood a cross, one
of the most grotesque forms of capital punishment ever
devised, and on that cross hung the holy Son of God, the
One that John the Baptist had referred to as "the Lamb of
God who takes away the sin of the world" (John 1:29).

What was He doing there? The Bible emphatically
states that He was paying the price that we might be
delivered from the evil bondage of sin. Years later, the
Apostle John explained it this way:

> And everyone who has this hope fixed on Him purifies
> Himself, just as He is pure. . . . And you know that He
> appeared in order to take away sins; and in Him there is
> no sin. . . . The Son of God appeared for this purpose, that
> He might destroy the works of the devil.

1 John 3:3, 5, 8

The problem of the ages can be summed up this way:
God is holy and will not tolerate sin in His Kingdom.
Therefore, one of two things must happen if we are to
have fellowship with Him. Either the sin in our lives will
go or we will go. Either sin can be dealt with, remedied,
and removed from our lives, or we will be removed from
the presence of the Holy One. The Apostle John declared
straightforwardly, "This is the message we have heard
from Him and announce to you, that God is light, and in

Him there is no darkness at all. If we say that we have fellowship with Him, and yet walk in the darkness, we lie and do not practice the truth" (1 John 1:5, 6).

Fortunately for us, God's heart broke over the problem long before ours did. He, therefore, set about devising a plan whereby purity could take on impurity, thus cleansing the unclean. God's answer to this horrible nightmare was to send His Son, Jesus Christ, to earth as a man, who lived a pure, perfect life and became the unblemished sacrifice for your sins and for mine.

Paul attempted to explain this concept to the Philippians when he encouraged them to have the same "attitude . . . which was also in Christ Jesus, who, although He existed in the form of God, did not regard equality with God a thing to be grasped, but emptied Himself, taking the form of a bond-servant, and being made in the likeness of men. And being found in appearance as a man, He humbled Himself by becoming obedient to the point of death, even death on a cross" (Philippians 2:5–8).

In the early 1950s, before the transplanting of human body organs became commonplace, a young boy developed a deadly kidney infection. Doctors worked around the clock in their attempt to save the young man, but all of their efforts produced nothing but failure. The boy's kidneys were so diseased, they could not possibly purify his system. There seemed to be no hope, nothing could be done, but to stand by helplessly and watch the boy die.

In desperation, one of the doctors suggested an idea to the dejected parents. "It's never been done before," he said hesitantly, "but if we can find a person whose blood type is the same as your son's, maybe . . . just maybe, we could run the blood of your boy through the system of the healthy person. Perhaps, if we proceeded slowly, taking just a little bit of the blood at a time, the kidneys of the healthy person could do the work that the boy's system cannot do."

"Let's try it!" the parents exclaimed almost simultaneously.

"You must understand. This has never been done before. We have no idea what will happen, and we cannot guarantee success. There is great risk involved here, for your son as well as to the donor," warned the doctor.

The parents looked hopefully at each other and nodded. "It's our only chance, doctor," the father answered. "Let's do it."

"All right, we must hurry. Does anyone here have the same blood type as the boy?"

"I do," said the dad.

"And you would be willing to volunteer?" the doctor asked, the concern evident in the tone of his voice.

"I will," responded the father.

"Do you understand the risks involved here?" the doctor implored.

"Yes, I do," the father answered soberly. "Let's get on with it."

Quickly, the medical staff tested the father's blood to make certain that it was the same type as the boy's. They prepped the father as if he were being operated upon, wheeled his gurney into the operating room, parked it parallel with his son's, and went to work.

They tenuously arranged tubing from the father to the son and back again, so the bodily system of the dad could take upon itself the impurities of his son, purifying the blood of the boy and returning him to health. As the process began to take effect, instantly, the father's temperature shot up. At the same time, slowly, the boy's fever began to recede, and his temperature came down. After a while, both the father and the son were out of critical danger and the operation was hailed as a huge success.

Seven days later, the boy was perfectly well and was released from the hospital, along with his father, to go home. The family was reunited for only two days when the father's temperature suddenly skyrocketed and, almost immediately, the father died.

The boy lived, but it cost the life of his dad. His father had taken upon himself the sickness, fever, disease, and death that rightfully had belonged to his child. Only one thing motivates a person to do something such as that— it's called *love*.

Though it is incomprehensible to our finite minds, something similar happened at Calvary, when Jesus took upon Himself our disease of sin. He who was absolutely pure took on our awful impurity. It cost Him His life, but as a result, we are able to live. The Apostle Paul summed it up: "He made Him who knew no sin to be sin on our behalf, that we might become the righteousness of God in Him" (2 Corinthians 5:21).

Consequently, God's wrath over sin does not have to be poured out upon us, because the blood of Jesus enables us to have a totally new relationship with Him. We are reconciled to God. His attitude toward us is one of amazing, unconditional love. Our attitude toward Him ought to be the same. When we accept His love—by acknowledging that Jesus paid the penalty for our sin with His blood, repenting of our sins, and seeking His forgiveness—we can be free from sin's deadly domination of our lives. Paul said, "Having now been justified by His blood, we shall be saved from the wrath of God through Him" (Romans 5:9).

The great hymnwriter, Charles Wesley, put it this way in his classic "And Can It Be":

And can it be that I should gain.
An int'rest in the Savior's blood?
Died He for me, who caused His pain?
For me, who Him to death pursued?
Amazing love! how can it be
That thou, my God, shouldst die for me?
Amazing love! how can it be
That Thou, my God, shouldst die for me?

The blood of Jesus makes it possible for a person's heart to be pure in God's sight, and this purity is an integral part of holiness.

4

What Positive
Holiness Is Not

A saintly gentleman approached me after I had taught a Bible study on the subject of holiness. With a twinkle in his eye, he said, "If you think about it, sometimes it's easier to understand what holiness is *not*, than what it is."

I've thought about it, and I think he is right. At the risk of compromising the title of this book, let me clear out some of the confusing clutter surrounding the subject.

First, holiness is not a state of ecstatic, emotional euphoria. It is not some spiritual experience into which you enter, after which you live in perpetual, overwhelming happiness. Although a holy person may approach life with a "heavenly" attitude, holiness is not heaven on earth.

Jesus was holy, yet He experienced sorrow, grief, and great pain. He hurt. He cried. He bled. He died.

A preacher known for his great faith telephoned me on a Saturday night, begging me to preach to his congregation on Sunday morning. Apparently, he had come down with a cold, but he didn't want his congregation to know, because he feared that they would interpret his sickness as an indication of weak faith. His faith may not have been weak, but his thinking certainly was!

Holiness is not a bubble in which you bounce merrily along from one "spiritual high" or "mountaintop experience" to the next, immune to the maladies of everyday life. Study the Scriptures and read the history of God's holiest saints, and you may be surprised at how many of them suffered intense physical and emotional stress. Paul, for example, had to live with what he called "a thorn in the flesh" (2 Corinthians 12:7–10). Many Bible scholars believe Paul's pain was caused by a physical infirmity. Furthermore, the Apostle's personal testimony (2 Corinthians 11:23–28) reads as though it were composed by a screenwriter for a grade-B horror movie. The man was imprisoned, beaten with rods, scourged with the feared cat-o'-nine-tails, stoned, shipwrecked, threatened by cold and exposure, and weighed down with incredible pressure from his spiritual responsibilities. Yet he regarded his struggle as merely "light affliction" (2 Corinthians 4:17) and hardly worth mentioning in comparison to the joys of knowing Jesus Christ and living in relationship with Him.

David Brainerd was a holy man who experienced almost intolerable hardships in his mission to the American Indians several decades before the colonies became a nation. Brainerd's biography, penned by the powerful preacher and scholar Jonathan Edwards, reveals the missionary's deep mental, emotional, physical, and spiritual struggles. The account produced a profound impact upon

John Wesley and, later, upon another great scholar and preacher, the founder of Gordon College, Adoniram Judson Gordon. Dr. Gordon often said that the book describing Brainerd's personal battles had influenced his life more than any other book besides the Bible.

Unquestionably, Brainerd's objectives in life were holiness of heart and service to his Savior. In his journal he said, "I long for God, and a conformity to His will, in inward holiness, ten thousand times more than for anything here below. . . . It was my meat and drink to be holy, to live to the Lord, and die to the Lord."[1] Still, the missionary was made to endure horrible difficulties in his labors for the Lord, and he died an early death. Holiness was not an escape hatch for David Brainerd.

Anyone who believes that holiness means freedom from affliction has obviously never read the Bible. The pages of Scripture are replete with illustrations of saintly individuals who experienced the perplexing and distressing pressures of life. Joseph, Job, and Daniel are but a few examples.

Joseph is one of the rare men in the Bible about whom there is not a negative word recorded concerning his adult life. Apparently, once he got past his problem with pride (remember his arrogance over his coat of many colors?), he proceeded to develop into the man God wanted him to be. Nevertheless, his holiness did not negate his trials and tribulations. In fact, because he was a holy man, he encountered terrible troubles in Egypt.

The Bible pictures Job as a perfect man, but in one day, he lost everything he possessed or loved dearly. His property, his priceless possessions, his children, and even his sense of personal pride were all destroyed by the devil's determined efforts to dethrone God as the Lord of Job's life. Still, Job continued to trust. While his wife whined, and his three infamous friends foolishly tried to figure out where Job had failed in his faith, the saint remained stalwart. In the midst of unimaginable desolation, Job declared his undying devotion to God: "Though He slay me, I will hope in Him . . ." (Job 13:15).

Daniel is another good example of a saint whose personal holiness got him in trouble. We are often quick to comment, "Daniel's faith in God delivered him out of the lion's den." True, but remember, as Tim Hansel says in his book *Holy Sweat*, it was Daniel's faith in God that got him *into* the lion's den, as well!

Holiness does not necessarily remove you from physical hindrances and hardships; neither does it necessarily enhance your mental and emotional capabilities.

In fairness, it must be acknowledged that many individuals *have* found their mental and emotional states to be dramatically affected by the changes brought about by the Holy Spirit in their lives. This should be expected since the Spirit renews our minds. Often, people of relatively average intelligence and mediocre abilities have been able to accomplish great things for God, once they have been empowered by the Holy Spirit. This is consistent with Scripture. In the Bible, God often chose ordinary men and women, filled them with His Spirit, and then used them to carry out spectacular tasks. Of course, the Spirit of God motivates myriads of men and women to do common, ordinary deeds, as well.

Nevertheless, holiness primarily produces perfect hearts, not necessarily perfect heads. Consequently, even holy men and women sometimes do dumb things. The saintliest Christian may say something extremely ignorant or make a stupid mistake. Holiness does not guarantee your entrance into the "High I. Q. Club." Nor is it the equivalent of an "Evelyn Wood Speed Reading Course," or a four-year education in biblical theology.

It is only logical, however, that if you are free from the tyranny of self-interest and you are under the wise, loving control of the Holy Spirit, you will be able to think much more clearly, thus maximizing your potential. The same is true in the emotional realm. If your self-image has been renewed by the Holy One, and you are free from the stress and insecurities formerly caused by sin in your life, you will undoubtedly function more fully as a human being. But be careful here—God will never take away your free will and turn you into a robot, nor will He remove from your shoulders the burden of responsibility for wise decisions. If you want to be holy, you must choose to place yourself under His Spirit's control, and then follow the instructions that He provides.

Furthermore, even when a person is holy, he or she will not cease to be fully human. Holiness does not transform you into Superman or Superwoman. If you are a bright person before you are filled with the Holy Spirit, it is safe to assume that you will be equally as bright after you begin your life of holiness, but not necessarily brighter. Similarly, if you are a gifted or creative individual before surrendering control of your life to Christ, you will probably continue to be talented in those areas, but not necessarily more adept.

Two important changes do take place, however, when a person enters into holiness. First, your heart and mind become illumined by the Spirit of Truth, and as a result, you may see and understand the world from a different perspective. You will begin to develop an eternal outlook; in some measure, you will start to see things as God sees them. Second, your intelligence, abilities, gifts, talents, and creativity are all part of your personhood that is submitted to the Holy Spirit. In a real sense, you no longer *possess* these attributes; they are His, to be used in and through you to glorify Jesus Christ. You have become the steward of those resources rather than the owner.

You may be wondering, *If holiness does not keep me from making mistakes, how can I tell the difference between normal human error and sin?* Much of the answer to that question comes down to the matter of motivation. Simply put, a mistake is involuntary, sin is voluntary.

An old story aptly illustrates this truth. A little boy helped his father to carefully select some onions that were ready to be picked from their garden. After they pulled the onions, the father and son washed, sorted, and laid them out to dry on the back porch.

"Good job, Son," the father said, as he gently patted his boy on the back. "Thanks for helping me to pull the onions."

Later that month, the boy was out in the garden by himself, when to his amazement, he discovered more onions growing in the same patch where he and his dad had already picked the onions previously!

Oh, boy! Dad's gonna love this! he thought, and he hastily proceeded to pull the pungent, edible bulbs from the ground. As he washed them under the spigot, the boy noticed that these onions were not nearly as large as the ones he and his dad had picked a few weeks earlier. Still, he couldn't wait to see his father's face when he saw this surprise.

When the father arrived home from work, the boy met him at the door. "Dad! Quick, come here. Look what I found out in the garden today!" he chirped enthusiastically.

His father allowed the boy to pull him through the kitchen and out onto the back porch. There, the man's countenance fell and his smile turned to a scowl.

"What's wrong, Dad? Look at the onions I found. Didn't I do good? Look, I cleaned them just like we did the other ones."

"Son, these onions aren't ready to be picked yet," the father answered soberly. "While you were at school, I replanted that part of the garden so we could have some more onions before the end of the summer. Now, they are ruined, and it's too late in the year to plant any more. I appreciate your work, and I know you meant well, but your actions were wrong."

Now, here's the question: Did the boy sin? Or did he merely make a mistake? Legalists and those who are strong supporters of harsh, holy justice would say, "Yes, the child acted wrongly and must be punished." They only see one facet of God's holiness. They rightly understand Him to be the Holy Judge; as such, they picture God as presiding over a courtroom. However, that which is considered wrong and punishable in a court of law is not always viewed as a violation in a family environment. Therefore, those who understand that God is not only our Holy Sovereign, He is also our heavenly Father, would say, "No, the boy's heart was clean. His motives were pure. Granted, he made a mistake, but it was not a voluntary, deliberate choice against his father's will. In fact, he had hoped to please his father by his actions."

In the same sense that a parent corrects a child who has done something wrong out of pure motives, God disciplines those whom He loves. Of course, He could not allow sin to go unpunished. His holiness demanded the cross of Christ, but always remember: It was His love that provided for the cross.

To say that holiness is a euphoric, perpetual state of cloud-nine experiences is utter foolishness. You will encounter grief, sorrow, and pain. You may make some serious errors. But despite perplexities, you can still have a peace that passes understanding. And in the midst of mistakes, it is possible to remain pure in motive.

Who Says Holy People Aren't Tempted?

Some people mistakenly believe that once a person enters into a holy life-style, he or she no longer must fight temptation. Nothing could be further from the truth! Holiness is not the absence of temptation; in actuality, it is the truly holy person who undergoes the fiercest assaults from Satan and his demonic forces.

Many people do not understand this simple truth and are surprised when they are severely tempted subsequent to having been filled with the Holy Spirit. If they succumb to temptations, some saints are shattered.

One man confessed his naiveté, "I never dreamed that I would have to deal with such difficult temptations even after my heart was cleansed! Fortunately, I found that verse, 1 Corinthians 10:13, where God said that He would never allow me to be tempted more than I could stand, and with the temptation, He would make a way of escape. Not only has He made a way for me to elude the enemy, He has given me the power to take that path when He has provided it."

Similar to a recovering alcoholic, who lives with the knowledge that he or she is only one drink away from addiction, the saint is always only one sin away from spiritual declension. Any time a Christian lets down his or her spiritual guard, or attempts to stand against Satan's temptation under his or her own stamina, you can be certain of negative results.

It may shock you to realize, but the "holier" you are, the more your temptations intensify, often plaguing you for prolonged periods of time. For example, Jesus, fresh from His anointing by the Holy Spirit, immediately was forced to face Satan in a series of profound temptations over a period of forty days. Apparently, He was further tempted throughout His life, as the Bible says, He was "tempted in all things as we are, yet without sin" (Hebrews 4:15).

Either you are holy or you're not.

Similarly, prior to Pentecost, the disciples were "living on easy street." They encountered little persecution, poverty, or imprisonment. After they were filled with the Holy Spirit, however, all of hell literally broke loose upon them. Suddenly, they were thrust into every sort of temptation and their faith was sorely tried.

Why does it work this way? Wouldn't you think that when a person is empowered by the supernatural Spirit of God, he or she is no longer susceptible to Satan's ploys? At least three truths counteract that logic.

First, the devil, knowing what immense value a holy person represents to the Kingdom of God, will do *anything* to squelch your quest for holiness. As soon as you begin seeking a deeper walk with the Lord, the devil launches an all-out onslaught in your direction. He will surround you with tempting opportunities, waging his strongest war at your weakest point, hoping to cause you to compromise or otherwise renege on your commitment to Christ. Satan saves his most severe temptations for the most sincere saints.

Second, the more similar in character you become to Jesus, the more you find even the appearance of evil to be abhorrent. Before you came to trust Christ as your Savior, you may have been able to indulge in sin with relative ease and impunity. After you came to know Him, things that never bothered you before suddenly loomed large, and you had an intense desire to be rid of those things that were not compatible with Christ. When He fills you with His Holy Presence, anything that is unholy or inconsistent with His holiness is sure to agitate you. Slight areas of compromise that previously seemed insignificant or inconsequential now are intolerable.

As such, temptations begin to take a different tack. At this point, we expect that the enemy will pull out the heavy guns and blast away at your willpower to resist "the seven deadly sins." Wrong. The devil does exactly the opposite. It is not normally the so-called "big" sins against which a holy person must take special precautions. It is the subtle sin with which Satan attempts to sabotage the saint. Temptations to pride, self-righteousness, hidden lust, false humility, and a host of other "minor moral indiscretions" must be resisted regularly if a man or woman is to remain holy.

A third reason why temptations are more intense for the Spirit-filled Christian is this: The saint is more *sensitized* to holiness, and is therefore also more sensitized to sin and its temptations. Think carefully about this: It is only the person who knows what purity is who can be tempted to be impure. For the callous, uncaring, unregenerate person, impurity is the norm. There is nothing tempting about it.

Similarly, it may well be the person with the highest appreciation for the glorious gift of human sexuality, and who knows the meaning of true love, who is most susceptible to temptations toward sexual immorality and lust. The saint is sensitized to both the holy and to the sinful. For the perverted or the promiscuous person, there

is little temptation associated with their immoral practices. They merely yield to their animalistic desires, and
do what comes naturally to a person who is lacking in
self-control.

If you think of temptation in that sense, then undoubtedly the Person who was most sensitized to sin must have
been Jesus Christ while He was here on earth, since He
was certainly sensitized to holiness. Imagine, then, the
horror of Calvary's cross, when He who was more sensitized to sin than any person in history, He who knew
better than any other the damning destructiveness of sin,
willingly took upon Himself the weight of the whole
world's sinfulness. Talk about a heavy thought!

Holiness Is Not Nirvana

Some religions teach that you can reach such a state of
spiritual perfection and bliss in this life that you need not
grow any further; you cease to sin; you cease striving; you
simply exist; you just are (whatever that means). Christianity, however, is not one of those religions. Holiness is
not simply an experience to be sought; it is a life to be
lived. It is not a magic carpet that you must force your
way onto, after which you can sit back and comfortably
coast on your way to heaven.

Recently, I listened with great interest as a famous
Bible teacher was speaking about Christ's Kingdom being
established here and now on earth. I could agree with
some of his message, but most of his presentation left me
perplexed. He gave the impression that he had "arrived"
spiritually.

"There is a Kingdom," he said dramatically, "and I
have entered into it." As he spoke, he stretched out his
arms and leaned back on his heels, as though attempting

to defy the forces of gravity; he flung his head backwards, shut his eyes, and whispered slowly, "I can see it. Yes. I see it. I'm walking into it. You can enter it, too! Come along. Come! Come into the Kingdom of God."

At first, I thought I had mistakenly stepped into the wrong room. I wasn't sure whether I was listening to a premier Gospel preacher or a guru expounding the latest twist on transcendental meditation. To my astonishment, he continued to imply that he had experienced a type of perfection not mentioned in the Bible. He clearly hinted at the claim that he no longer sinned. Furthermore, he could not remember the last time he had been sick, "it was so many years ago." He had been delivered, he said, from all lusts, regrets, questions, and doubts in his spiritual life. Neither had he suffered any financial setbacks, personal humiliations, or mistakes in judgment. The longer I listened, the more I thought, *Who is this guy trying to kid?* Unfortunately, the audience bought it.

Such a charade is an unbiblical sham of holiness. Granted, when a person's heart is cleansed and he or she is filled with the Holy Spirit, in what theologians refer to as a *crisis experience,* it does seem as though you have entered into a new dimension of deeper spiritual living. Nevertheless, no matter how many giant steps forward you take in your journey, you can never stop growing. That's what theologians refer to as a *progressive spiritual experience.*

For example, when a couple says "I do" on their wedding day, those few puffs of air totally transform their lives. Their wedding is the crisis experience in which they commit themselves to each other in marriage. The ceremony and accompanying celebration may last a few minutes, or in some extreme cases, a few days.

A wedding, however, does not make a marriage. The

couple then must go out and bond together as husband and wife. That is the progressive part, in which they live, learn, love, and grow together. If, after the vows were stated, the pronouncement made, the pictures taken, and the cake all eaten, the couple then said, "Okay, that's that. We've got a handle on this marriage thing," it would be ludicrous.

Yet, strangely that kind of foolish reasoning prevails in some Christian circles. It is as though once a person has reached a particular spiritual plateau, or has had a certain experience, he or she has "arrived." They are spiritual, or as it may be piously pronounced, "spid-i-chull" (with the tongue stuck to the top of your upper teeth).

The truly holy person is never content to be "spid-i-chull." Sincere saints quickly become uncomfortable with status quo spiritual lives. They want to grow. They are excited about seeking a richer, deeper relationship with the Lord Jesus. He, in turn, is constantly molding and shaping them, by His Spirit, into His own image. He continues to expand their horizons, to illumine their minds with new ideas and insights, and to open to them vast vistas of spiritual possibilities they had previously never imagined, let alone explored.

While peace is the permanent property of the Spirit-filled person, holy living should never be confused as static, stationary, or inert. You must continue to press on, even after you have entered into holiness. Keep learning new lessons; keep growing in grace and knowledge of the truth; and keep bringing forth more and better spiritual fruit in your life.

The Apostle Paul was certainly a saint, but he refused to adopt an arrogant, self-righteous "I have arrived" attitude. Speaking of all the riches that Christ had in store for him, Paul said, "Not that I have already obtained it, or have already become perfect, but I press on in order that I may lay hold of that for which also I was laid hold of by Christ Jesus. Brethren, I do not regard myself as having laid hold of it yet; but. . . . I press on toward the goal for the prize of the upward call of God in Christ Jesus" (Philippians 3:12–14).

Then Paul pitches us a curve. Immediately after proclaiming that he is not yet perfect, he says, "Let us therefore, *as many as are perfect*, have this attitude . . ." (Philippians 3:15, *italics mine*). He continues: ". . . if in anything you have a different attitude, God will reveal that also to you; however, let us keep living by the same standard to which we have attained" (3:15, 16). Wait a minute! What's going on here? Has Paul flipped his apostolic lid? No. He is simply saying, "I'm not in heaven yet, but I have experienced a measure of spiritual maturity. Still, I'm going to keep living in holiness, and I'm pressing on for more!" He was so confident of his direction, Paul declared to the Corinthians, "Be imitators of me, just as I also am of Christ" (1 Corinthians 11:1). By implication, he was saying, "If you want to see what a holy, Christ-like life is all about, watch me!" Most of us shudder at the thought of saying something similar to that. We shun scrutiny of our personal lives, but to Paul such surveillance and emulation made perfect sense.

Imperfectly Perfect

Because of Paul's use of the term *perfect*, many people have confused holiness as "sinless perfection." This may be the quickest and sharpest rebuke you will receive if you begin to talk seriously about being holy in this lifetime. "Do you mean that you never sin?" people will ask you in either amazement, amusement, or anger. Our spiritual forefathers, however, were not fools. They understood precisely what they were talking about when they used such terminology. Unfortunately, semantics are not always stable signposts; they are usually in a state of flux. As such, when we read the words of the great saints from past generations, we sometimes invest their thoughts with our modern interpretations, which may not be consistent with their original intentions.

Nevertheless, if there is one truth about holiness upon which most spiritual giants agree, it is this: Holiness is not a state from which you cannot fall. It is unscriptural and extremely dangerous to assume that there is any state of spiritual grace that can be attained in this lifetime, from which you *cannot* fall.

John Wesley, considered by many to be the "Father of Christian Perfection," was quite clear when he was questioned about this matter. He said, "There is no such height or strength of holiness as it is impossible to fall from."[2]

Understand, however, a holy person does not need to fall. All of the enormous power of the Holy Spirit is available to keep a person from falling into sin. Nevertheless, we stand only by faith (Romans 11:16–22) and Paul warns, "Therefore let him who thinks he stands take heed lest he fall" (1 Corinthians 10:12).

How can a holy man or woman fall? I don't know. How could Lucifer and the other angels who lived in the very presence of God fall into sin? How could Adam and Eve, living in a perfect environment, the idyllic Garden of Eden, rebel against God? How could great saints in the Scriptures and down through human history disavow knowledge of their King and disobey His Word? How could pastors, Sunday school teachers, television minis-

ters, and Christian musicians . . . and how could you fall
from grace?

How does it happen? Self-will. Usually, when a saint
bites the dust, it is due to the tyranny of self-interest
resurfacing in his or her life. Of course, it cannot come
back into play unless you allow it to do so, but have no
illusions, if you leave the door open just a crack, the devil
will be delighted to help you resurrect your crucified
self-life. If you choose to take back an area of your life that
you had formerly surrendered to Christ's control, the
Lord will relinquish the reins, but you will be dependent
upon your own strength in that area. And guess where
Satan is most likely to shoot the next dart of temptation?
Yep, right where you are most vulnerable—the place
where you have relied upon your own human resources,
rather than the supernatural power of Christ. Satan is not
invincible, but he is a formidable foe, and it is doubtful
that you will be able to stand against him, unprotected,
for long. At that point, you most likely will fall into sin.
If so, you will not sin because you must; you will sin
because of the choices you have made.

Can this sort of failure be prevented? Certainly! You
can continue to live a holy life, but you will have to keep
a close watch over your heart. Be sure it is wholly His.
Pray, read your Bible, fellowship with other believers,
and daily put on the full armor of God.

Don't be bashful about taking the necessary defensive
precautions by avoiding those things that you know from
past experiences are potential pitfalls for you. Keep in
mind, also, that you are still operating in hostile, enemy
territory, and that this Christian life is a battlefield, not a
playground.

Nevertheless, keep a positive attitude about your life.
Genuine holiness is always positive, exciting, and conta-

gious. It is love, rather than legalism. It is joy rather than judgmentalism. Positive holiness is dynamic and progressive, rather than stifling and static. It is always stretching, growing, seeking to be ever more like Jesus.

Perhaps the songwriter summed it up when he wrote:

> To be like Jesus,
> To be like Jesus!
> All I ask [is] to be like Him!
> All through life's journey
> From earth to glory,
> All I ask [is] to be like Him.

5

How Deep Is Your Love?

In the spring of 1968, my brother and I began a musical ministry known as The Watchmen Quartet, which later evolved into the contemporary Christian rock band ABRAHAM. In twenty years, we traveled several million miles and saw literally thousands of individuals respond to invitations to meet Jesus Christ. One of the keys to the effectiveness of our ministry took place when the group had barely begun.

One Sunday morning, we sang at a large Methodist church and the Spirit of the Lord moved mightily in the service. Afterwards, the pastor of the church invited us to have a meal with him and his wife. Basking in the success of the service, we gladly accepted.

The meal proceeded with the usual pleasantries and was relatively uneventful until the pastor put down his

eating utensils and leaned back in his chair at the head of
the table. He seemed to eye each of us suspiciously before
saying, "Yessir, I sure did enjoy that music this morning.
You boys did a fine job."

"Thank you, sir," one of us managed to squeeze out
through a mouthful of mashed potatoes.

"Yep, a fine job. You sing real well. Nice harmonies.
Beautiful blend. Marvelous melodies."

"We 'preciate it, Pastor."

"Mmm-mmmh. I'll bet you do. You write your own
songs, I assume?"

"Yes, sir; we do."

"I figured as much. Nice. Very nice."

We all kept eating as the pastor pulled up straight in his
chair, propped his elbows on the table, and placed his
chin on his hands before continuing. "Only one problem
I can see," he said as if he was speaking past us to an
unseen observer.

"Problem?" Everyone quit chewing almost simultaneously.

"Hmmm? Oh, yes. Problem," the pastor toyed with his
words until he was sure he had our attention. "Well,
maybe you could say it's just a question I have about your
music."

"What would that be, sir?" someone asked.

The pastor put his hands flat on the table and looked
around the room at each of us before answering, "I just
wonder who you are singing for. Are you really singing
for Jesus? Or are you singing for yourselves? For your own
pride. For your own ego trip."

I began to open my mouth to respond to the pastor's
questions, but it was obvious that he was not done
probing. It was probably providential that I kept silent
because his next words were prophetic and were to form

a cornerstone of our ministry for the next twenty years.

He said slowly and lovingly, "You see, boys, good singers are a dime a dozen. So are good songwriters. But holy, Spirit-filled singers and songwriters are extremely rare. God doesn't need your performance. If He was looking for performers, He could send a few thousand angels to do the job. He's looking for holy hearts. He wants you to be so surrendered to Him and clean before Him, that when you get up to sing or speak, people will know that they are not hearing your opinions or what you think; but they will know they are in the presence of a holy God, and hearing what He says."

That pastor has long since gone to be with the Lord, but he taught us that the key to effective Christian service is threefold: the cleansing of your heart, the surrender of your will, and being filled with the Holy Spirit. Over the years, I have often wished that his secret of spiritual success could have been preserved for posterity, for the benefit of future generations of Christian servants. Maybe now it will be.

Another musician whose words are worth reviewing was the remarkable nineteenth-century songwriter, Frances Ridley Havergal. Some of her classic hymns include "Take My Life and Let it Be" and "Like a River Glorious." Miss Havergal often acknowledged that the keys to her success were surrender and cleansing. On surrender, she said, "I saw it as a flash of electric light, and what you see you can never unsee. There must be full surrender before there can be full blessedness. God admits you by one into the other. . . . So I just yielded myself to Him and utterly trusted Him to keep me."[1]

Later she wrote of her own experience, "The wonderful and glorious blessing, which so many Christians are testifying to have found, was suddenly, marvelously, sent to me last winter; and life is now what I never imagined life on earth could be. . . ." Furthermore, Frances Havergal saw clearly that the cleansing blood of Jesus did a complete, purifying work in her heart. Basing her convictions upon the Scripture verse "the blood of Jesus . . . cleanses us from all sin" (1 John 1:7), Miss Havergal became convinced that not only did the blood of Jesus cleanse past sins, but believers could depend upon Christ's blood for continual cleansing.

She wrote to a friend,

> As to "perfectionism" or "sinlessness," I have all along, and over and over again, said I never did, and do not, hold either. . . . But being kept from falling, kept from sins, is quite another thing. The Bible seems to teem with commands and promises about it. . . . Have we not been limiting the cleansing power of the precious blood when applied by the Holy Spirit, and also the keeping power of our God? Have we not been limiting 1 John 1:7, by practically making it refer only to "the remission of sins that are past," instead of taking the grand simplicity of "cleanseth us from all sin?"
>
> "All" is all; and as we may trust Him to cleanse from the stain of past sins, so we may trust Him to cleanse from all present defilement. . . . It was that one word "cleanseth" which opened the door of a very glory of hope and joy to me.[2]

Throughout the Old Testament, cleanness and purity, both externally and internally, were prominent conditions of holiness. This is easily seen in Leviticus, where the terms *cleanness* and *holiness* are used almost synonymously. The idea was that only "clean" objects or people could accurately be called "holy."

In his well-known prayer of repentance after his adul-

terous affair with Bathsheba, King David related the
cleansing of his heart to his relationship with the Holy
Spirit. He prayed "Purify me with hyssop, and I shall be
clean; Wash me, and I shall be whiter than snow. . . .
Create in me a clean heart, O God, and renew a steadfast
spirit within me. Do not cast me away from Thy presence,
and do not take Thy Holy Spirit from me" (Psalms 51:7,
10, 11). Psalm 18 and Psalm 119 also refer to the purifying
work of the Holy Spirit.

Perhaps one of the most spiritually sublime Old Testament passages of Scripture linking holiness and purity
comes from the pen of the prophet Ezekiel. In a passage
that certainly applies to the future restoration of Israel,
but also has present ramifications for believers, God
spoke through Ezekiel:

> Then I will sprinkle clean water on you, and you will be
> clean; I will cleanse you from all your filthiness and from
> all your idols. Moreover, I will give you a new heart and
> put a new spirit within you; and I will remove the heart of
> stone from your flesh and give you a heart of flesh. And I
> will put My Spirit within you and cause you to walk in My
> statutes, and you will be careful to observe My ordi-
> nances.

> Ezekiel 36:25–27

In the New Testament, again the work of the Holy Spirit
is associated with cleansing and purifying. John the
Baptist set the pace when he boldly proclaimed, "I
baptize you with water for repentance, but He who is
coming after me is mightier than I, and I am not even fit
to remove His sandals; He will baptize you with the Holy
Spirit and fire. And His winnowing fork is in His hand,

and He will thoroughly clear His threshing floor; and He will gather His wheat into the barn, but He will burn up the chaff with unquenchable fire" (Matthew 3:11, 12). Ouch! Obviously, in John's mind, true followers of the Christ would either be *purified* by fire or *punished* by fire.

Chaos at the Church Conference

Maybe the Apostle Peter was mulling over these words in his mind as he listened to the opinions expressed at the "First Ecumenical Council of the Christian Church" held in Jerusalem about ten years after the Holy Spirit had been poured out on the Day of Pentecost. It was a tense meeting and the debate was hot and heavy. Much of the conflict centered around the issue of the new Gentile converts.

Some of the early Christians, especially those who were formerly associated with the sect of the Pharisees, wanted the Gentile believers to submit to the Jewish rites and rituals. They said, "It is necessary to circumcise them, and to direct them to observe the Law of Moses" (Acts 15:5) The former Pharisees had a dangerous tendency to transfer their legalistic practices from Judaism into their new-found faith. To them, holy Christian living meant "obey the rules."

Peter, however, found it difficult to accept that concept of Christianity. As he sat listening to the discussion, he was probably pondering what he and some of his friends from Joppa had just recently experienced in Caesarea. There, Peter had seen and heard with his own eyes and ears what God had done in the life of a Roman centurion named Cornelius.

Prior to his experiences at Cornelius's place, Peter had not been overly open to the idea of Gentile converts,

either. But while he was praying one day in Joppa, the
Lord graphically demonstrated to him in a vision that the
old distinctions were to be done away with. Three times
during his vision, Peter heard a voice command, "What
God has cleansed, no longer consider unholy" (Acts
10:15). Peter was perplexed. What did it all mean? Then,
while he was still reflecting on this incredible vision, the
Spirit informed Peter of the arrival of emissaries from
Cornelius and instructed the baffled disciple to accom-
pany them.

When Peter arrived at Cornelius's home, the centurion
briefly explained how God had divinely instructed him to
contact Peter and that he had gathered his entire family
and many of his close friends to hear what the Lord had
commanded Peter to say. Finally understanding that
"God is not one to show partiality," Peter began preaching
to them (see Acts 10:34).

Suddenly, an astonishing sequence of events occurred.
"While Peter was still speaking . . . the Holy Spirit fell
upon all those who were listening to the message" (Acts
10:44). Peter hadn't even finished his sermon! Nevertheless, the Holy Spirit was poured out upon the gathering at
Cornelius's house that day, and those Gentiles began
"speaking with tongues and exalting God" (10:46).

When Peter went back to Jerusalem, some of the Jewish
Christians took issue with him for taking the Gospel to
the Gentiles. But after Peter related to them his eyewitness
account of what had happened at Caesarea, they glorified
God and said, "Well then, God has granted to the Gentiles
also the repentance that leads to life" (Acts 11:18). From
that point on, Peter and the other leading disciples had
considered the case closed.

Now, here it was again, the cause of "great dissension
and debate" (Acts 15:2).

Peter sat quietly as the former Pharisees fussed over the future conditions of their fellowship. Finally, he could take it no longer. He stood up and said to them, " 'Brethren, you know that in the early days God made a choice among you, that by my mouth the Gentiles should hear the word of the gospel and believe. And God, who knows the heart, bore witness to them, giving them the Holy Spirit, just as He also did to us; and He made no distinction between us and them, cleansing their hearts by faith' " (Acts 15:7–9).

Peter's words were clear, kind, and concise, yet they cut straight to the heart of the matter. He stated in no uncertain terms that God had accepted those Gentiles who had believed the Gospel; how could anyone who called himself or herself a follower of Jesus do less? Furthermore—and here is where Peter's speech packed a powerful punch—the Gentiles acceptance was not contingent upon birth, race, adherence to religious rites or creeds, ecstatic experiences, or any other external differences. To Peter, the proof of prime importance was the fact that when Cornelius and his household were filled with the Holy Spirit, He purified their hearts by faith.

By implication, Peter condemned those Christians who still insisted upon clinging to rules and regulations, rites and rituals as external evidence of their holiness. Peter did not deny that external manifestations accompanied the outpouring of the Spirit. Obviously, Cornelius and his guests had spoken in "tongues" and had enthusiastically praised God (Acts 10:46). This phenomenon was not unfamiliar to Peter; he had experienced similar effects himself on several occasions. Nevertheless, he declared that God had done something even more significant: "He has cleansed their hearts by faith." Peter proclaimed that God's power, His presence, and His holy personality characteristics were available to any person who would allow himself or herself to be purified.

Dr. Donald Metz, an outstanding twentieth-century Bible scholar, has commented, "To the Early Church, inner purity rather than external evidence was the irreducible evidence of the baptism with the Holy Spirit. In practical experience this inner purity resulting from the baptism with the Holy Spirit is called the experience or state of holiness."[3]

It is this sense of inner purity that great Christians have sought down through the centuries. John Allan Wood, a godly pastor who preached in Binghamton, Massachusetts, just prior to the Civil War, is a good example. Although soundly converted at ten years of age, much of Wood's early Christian experience left him perplexed, distressed, and disappointed. When he decided to enter the ministry, his heart's sinful condition convicted him. Concerning the contradiction within himself, Wood wrote:

> I was often convicted of remaining corruption of heart and of my need of purity. I desired to be a decided Christian and a useful member of the church; but was often conscious of deep-rooted inward evils and tendencies in my heart unfriendly to godliness. My bosom-foes troubled me more than all my foes from without. They struggled for the ascendency. They were the instruments of severe temptation. They interrupted my communion with God. They crippled my efforts to do good. They invariably sided with Satan. They occupied a place in my heart which I knew should be possessed by the Holy Spirit. They were the greatest obstacles to my growth in grace, and rendered my service to God but partial.[4]

Just as Frances Havergal had done, Wood rejected any possibility of "sinless perfection" here on earth. He didn't even appreciate the biblical terms *holiness* and *sanctification*, which were prominent in the sermons of many of the popular preachers of his day. It agitated him greatly when he heard people give testimony to an experience of heart-cleansing that was subsequent to their initial salvation experience. In his preaching, Wood taught that holiness was only "a deeper work of grace, or a little more religion."

Still, Pastor Wood's heart hungered for a consistent experience of purity and power in his own life and in his ministry. In spite of his theological prejudices against it, Wood said, "Through the entire summer of 1858, I was seeking holiness, but kept the matter to myself. . . . God only knew the severe struggles I had that long summer, during many hours of which I lay on my face in my study, begging Jesus to cleanse my poor, unsanctified heart. . . ."[5]

In September of that year, Wood attended the Binghamton camp meeting, along with eighty members of his church. On the last day of the conference, one of Wood's most faithful church members went to the pastor weeping and confronted the preacher squarely about his spiritual condition.

He said, "Brother Wood, there is no use trying to dodge this question. You know your duty. If you will lead the way, and define your position as a seeker of entire sanctification, you will find that many of the members of your charge have a mind to do the same."

Humbled first by the Lord, and now through this direct confrontation with a faithful member of his congregation, Pastor Wood conceded. He replied, "Immediately after preaching I will appoint a meeting in our tent on the subject of holiness, and will ask the prayers of the Church for my own soul."

That humble admission of need was the turning point

for Pastor Wood. He said later, "In an instant I felt a giving away in my heart so sensible and powerful that it appeared physical rather than spiritual; a moment after I felt an indescribable sweetness permeating my entire being. . . . I was conscious that Jesus had me in His arms, and that the Heaven of heavens was streaming through and through my soul in such beams of light and overwhelming love and glory, as can never be uttered."

In describing his experience, Pastor Wood recognized that his holiness was derived from God and that it was not something he had accomplished through his own self-effort. He commented, "After I reached that point of complete submission, I had no consciousness of making any special effort in believing; my whole being seemed simply, and without effort, to be borne away to Jesus."

Furthermore, his sanctification was not limited to a single, euphoric experience. His entire Christian life and ministry continued to be transformed.

> From that hour the deep and solid communion with God, and the rich baptisms of love and power have been "unspeakable and full of glory". . . . There was a divine fragrance and sweetness imparted to my soul when the Savior cleansed and filled it with pure love, that has ever remained with me, and I trust it ever will. . . . To know that God is mine; to feel that He dwells in my heart, rules my will, my affections, my desires; to know that He loves me ten thousand times better than I love Him—oh, what solid bliss is this![6]

Pastor Wood experienced what I call "positive holiness." He discovered, as you can, that true holiness is not constricting, but liberating; it will not make you spiritually, emotionally, or psychologically impotent; it will empower you to live successfully as a Christian in a markedly unchristian world. Positive holiness is not more baggage you must lug through life; it is the cleansing and purifying of the binding sin that has kept you from being what God intends you to be.

Andrew Murray, the beloved devotional writer from South Africa, often pointed out this concept of positive holiness. Holiness is more than cleansing, Murray said, but holiness must be preceded by purity. He wrote, "The cleansing is the negative side, the being separate and not touching the unclean thing, the removal of impurity; the sanctifying is the positive union and fellowship with God, and the participation of the graces of the divine life and holiness. . . . Cleansing must ever prepare the way, and ought always to lead on to holiness."[7]

If that is so, and it is, let's move on to see how positive holiness can become the consistent testimony of your life.

Overcoming
Spiritual Impotence

Some days it seems you shouldn't even bother to get out of bed. You know how it goes: You jump out of bed in the morning, or perhaps, more likely you *slide* out from under the covers, semi-excited to meet the day. You prepare your heart and mind by reading a bit of the Bible and talking with God in prayer, and you're off to a great start. Then what happens?

Inevitably, you encounter one of those arrogant, contentious, obnoxious, demanding, impatient individuals whose apparent mission in life is to test *your* patience or try *your* nerves. Suddenly, your whole day is shot. Your peace with God is ruined. You find yourself hurt, angry, bitter, confused, or experiencing any number of other negative emotions and attitudes that you just got done praying about!

Disgusted and discouraged, you cry out, "How am I supposed to live a consistent Christian life in this un-christian world?"

Here's another situation: You go to church and joyfully praise and worship the Lord. After the service, you walk out feeling great, spiritually refreshed, and ready to take the world for Jesus. Then, first thing you know, you get angry with someone at home. Maybe the kids get to you; or possibly your spouse, brother, sister, mom or dad, or the neighbor does something to bug you; or you lose your temper at work. Or you yield to an immoral habit that you thought you had beaten. Or you get tangled up in some sinful attitude or action that you just can't seem to overcome.

Exasperated, you wonder, "Is there any hope for me? How long will I flounder in this utter futility and failure? Is this the best I can be? Am I honestly expected to be holy? Are You serious, God?"

Scripture makes it extremely clear that consistent, Christ-like living is more than a mere pipe dream. You can walk in love and obedience. Furthermore, God expects us to live holy lives. He commands it! Remember, "You shall be holy, for I am holy." Not only does He demand it, but here's the good news: He also promises us that positive holiness is *possible* for every believer. We are *not* to live in perpetual failure. As Paul says in Romans 6:14, sin shall *not* be your master!

If holiness is so important to God, and so crucial to our Christian lives, why don't we experience it more consistently? Why are so many believers losing the battle in their struggle against sin? Why does the Church of Jesus Christ so often seem to be more conformed to this world than it is to the Holy God we claim to know, love, and serve?

One reason for our spiritual impotence is our spiritual ignorance. Many people who have been Christians for years are still confused, misguided, or misinformed when it comes to the matter of personal holiness.

Some Common Misconceptions

Most of us don't have any problem with the idea of *God* being holy. He is *supposed* to be holy! After all, He's God! Similarly, most people don't mind talking about the Holy *Bible*. Some people will even talk about the *Church* as being holy. But when we start talking about *you* being holy . . . Oh! That's a different story! If you are like many, your first response is, "Who me? Holy? What do you think I am, a saint?" At this point, the biblical writers would answer emphatically: "*Yes!* That is exactly what you are to be."

To be a saint does not imply that you are ready to be made into a statue and placed upon somebody's dashboard or fireplace mantle. Sainthood is the normal status for all genuine followers of Jesus Christ. In the New Testament, the most common name ascribed to Christian believers is *saints*. The word means "holy ones," or "those consecrated unto God," and is most often used in the Book of Acts, after the Holy Spirit was poured out on the Day of Pentecost. It is also prominent in Paul's letters, even though not all of those to whom Paul referred as saints were, in fact, saintly in character.

Today, most Christians squirm uncomfortably if they are referred to as saints. The term has been elevated to infer a sort of superspiritual status, as the original meaning of the word *saint* has largely fallen into disuse. Scripturally, however, you could legitimately greet your fellow believers by saying, "Hello there, Saint Natalie," or "Hi, Saint Eric," and the attribution would be perfectly appropriate.

Interestingly, the word *saint* comes from the same words in Hebrew (*qadosh*) and Greek (*hagios*) that are most often translated "holy". The words *sanctify* and *sanctification* also come from these roots. The implication is that holiness, or saintliness, is not restricted to an isolated few super-Christians, but should be the normal common denominator of all true believers.

Admittedly, the concept of holiness seems a bit archaic to this current generation of Christians. Most people think that holiness has something to do with the condemnation of external adornments or unnecessary accoutrements in our already overly indulgent life-styles. Ask most Christians what it means to be holy, and almost invariably they will begin mumbling about externals. They will point you to particular hairstyles, manners of dress, or social mores that they have associated with holiness.

I recall the first time I attended a conference on the subject of holiness. I was barely eighteen years old and a relatively new Christian. Still I couldn't help noticing the "acceptable" looks and the "unacceptable" appearances among the attendees. Most of the women, I discovered, dressed in long-sleeved, drab-colored outfits (though dark skirts and white blouses seemed to have made the "acceptable" list). Few of the women wore any makeup, and those who dared applied the color sparingly.

The "acceptable" attire for men struck me as being equally bland. Most of the fellows conformed by dressing in boring black or blue suits, with the more daring among them opting for brackish browns or grisly grays. Anything that vaguely hinted at being stylish or fashionable was viewed askance by the conferees and considered to be worldly.

I was most amazed by the women's hairstyles. After close observation, I was able to categorize them into three acceptable coiffures: the Bun, the Beehive, and the Beaver. The Bun was popular, it seemed, with the older women, since it only required a woman to sweep her hair onto her head and then pin it down with as many hairpins as necessary. The Beehive was the favorite among the middle-aged women. Hair was pitched high upon a woman's head, ascending into a precarious spiral, until it became a Leaning Tower of Pisa of hair. The Beaver beat them both, in my opinion. The Beaver was a pile of hair slung backwards over a woman's head, running down her back and restrained in a huge hairnet. It looked as though a large animal was attacking the woman from behind.

Needless to say, my first impressions of holiness were not positive. Ironically, my preoccupation with the appearances of the attendees caused me to totally miss the point of the conference. What those well-meaning conferees regarded as external evidence of their piety had confused me and conveyed an anachronistic and inaccurate impression of holiness. Oddly, the concentration upon the externals created an obstacle that caused me to miss the true, *internal* aspects of heart-cleansing holiness.

Please understand, it is your right to wear your hair in any particular style you choose—but there is nothing more or less holy about a hairstyle. Similarly, if you prefer a pale face, devoid of makeup, or dark, drab clothing, *viva la difference!* If that is your preference, press on; but *please* don't confuse that with holiness.

On the other extreme, at a recent Christian rock concert, a musician friend asked me a curious question. "Ken," he asked seriously, "can a Christian punk-rocker be a holy person?"

"What do you mean by a punk-rocker?" I asked.

"You know, someone who wears his hair in a pretty weird style and dresses in wild clothes and plays loud, raucous, rock 'n' roll music," he answered, laughing as he spoke.

"As I understand it, holiness has to do with a person's heart, not his or her hair," I replied. "As for the clothes and the music, there is just no accounting for some people's tastes!"

Our external appearances and conduct are constantly making statements concerning our allegiances. We need to keep in mind at all times that we are representing the King of kings and Lord of lords. Still, we err grievously when we place our emphasis upon external evidences of our holiness. Unfortunately, this mistake has been one of the most frequent and most harmful hindrances to true holiness in many lives.

Other people equate holiness with a long list of prohibitions. They make trifling remarks such as, "I don't do drugs, go to movies, dance, or listen to secular music," or "I don't drink, smoke, chew, or run around with girls who do!" The list goes on and on. Notice again that the emphasis is upon the negative and upon the externals. This is psuedo-holiness.

Perhaps more serious is the corollary that logically results from such negativism. People begin to assume that holiness means developing a self-righteous "holier-than-thou" attitude. Unfortunately, they are usually quick to tell you how much holier-than-thou they really are!

On the other hand, many people view holiness as an unattainable perfection. They see it as something God said you should shoot for, but *He* knows and *you* know that you're never going to make it, that you are never going to hit the mark or achieve the goal. Therefore, you might as well not even try to live up to His standards. As a result of this half-truth, many devout Christians have condemned themselves to lives of failure and frustration, delusion and discouragement. They have been duped into believing that no matter what effort they put forth, it is impossible for them to ever please God.

Of course it is impossible to live up to God's standards on your own strength. Maybe that is why He never asked you to do so. The Word is clear that it is " 'Not by might nor by power, but by My Spirit,' says the Lord of hosts" (Zechariah 4:6), that any work of true eternal value will be accomplished. Never underestimate the power of the Holy Spirit to shape you into the holy person He has called you to be.

Maybe you have assimilated one or more of these misconceptions and negative mental images of a holy person. Allow me to gently remind you that all of these ideas miss the mark when it comes to the true meaning of holiness.

To be holy is to be *morally blameless*. It is to be separated *from* sin and consecrated (totally dedicated) *to* God. As we have discovered, holiness includes:

1. A radiant brightness.
2. Being set apart for God's use and for God's glory.
3. Purity, living unspotted by the world and having a clean heart before God.

Then Why Don't We Do It?

In his book *Pursuit of Holiness*, Jerry Bridges offers another theory to explain the dichotomy between what modern disciples of Christ *say* they believe, and how they actually live. Our problem, says Bridges, "is that our attitude toward sin is usually more self-centered than God-centered."[1]

Most of us are more concerned about our own spiritual *success* than we are about the fact that our sins grieve the heart of God. We're more concerned about how bad we feel, how deeply our guilt and shame have hurt us, than we are that our sins make the blood of Jesus Christ a mockery, that we insult the Holy Spirit of grace every time we willfully continue to sin (Hebrews 10:26, 29). Nowadays, we worry about failure, discomfort, or dysfunction in our lives as a result of sin, but few of us dread sin because we know that it is an offense to God.

An unmarried man who claimed to be a Christian confided to me that he finally was able to stop having premarital sex ever since the public scare over AIDS and herpes.

My curiosity was piqued, so I asked, "Are you more afraid of getting AIDS or of offending God?"

"I guess I am more afraid of AIDS," he replied matter-of-factly. We talked further and I got the impression that if it wasn't for the fear of disease, he would continue right on sinning with impunity!

Most of us are like that. We're not concerned about sinning, we're concerned about getting caught! Do you live the way you do because you love God and want to please Him, or do you do the things you do (or don't do) because you're scared to death that He is going to punish you, either here on earth or by sending you to hell forever?

Many Christians think lightly of sin; consequently, they have a commensurate esteem for the holiness of God. But you will never truly comprehend and experience

God's holiness until you grasp how much He hates sin. Understand, all sin is against God. It is like spitting in Jesus' face! It is *His* law that you are breaking. It is *His* authority that you are rebelling against. It is *His* character that you are despising. It is *His* Kingdom that you are undermining, sabotaging, and selling out as a traitor.

Repentance of sin requires much more than merely feeling sorry for ourselves and despairing over our plight. We tend to think that admittance of our failure is all that is necessary, that we can simply pray a few remorseful words or shed a few tears and everything will be fine. Oh, no it won't! That sort of repentance is inadequate; it will never do!

True repentance demands a complete turning away from sin, a renouncement of it, an irrevocable desire to be done with it. Let me remind you that Pharaoh, Balaam, Saul, and Judas all admitted that they had sinned. Each of them said, "I've done wrong and I have sinned!" But they did not repent and change their way of thinking, acting, or living! They were not concerned that they had offended the holy Lord God. They were only embarrassed and discouraged because they had failed, that things hadn't worked out the way they had planned.

On the other hand, think of the story of the prodigal son. He said, "I will get up, go back, and say, 'Father, I have sinned against heaven, and in your sight!' " He was forgiven (Luke 15:11–32). Or think about David. He had sinned with Bathsheba and had ordered her husband, Uriah, to be murdered. Furthermore, he had hidden his sin for nearly a year before he was confronted by the prophet Nathan. Nevertheless, when David honestly repented, he was forgiven. Sadly, the consequences of his sin plagued him for the rest of his life, but at least David's heart was clean and his relationship with the Lord was restored (2 Samuel 12:13).

Another reason why so few Christians ever press on into holy Christian living, according to Bridges, is that we have misunderstood this whole matter of living by faith. I agree with this assessment and would expand it to include what some present-day teachers are calling the "faith-walk." At one extreme of the faith and holiness spectrum, you will find many who believe that no effort at all is required on our part to live a life of holiness. Bridges points out, "Sometimes we have even suggested that any effort on our part is 'of the flesh.' "[2] At the other extreme, some modern faith and prosperity teachers, who are quick to quote, "This is the victory that has overcome the world—our faith" (1 John 5:4), often give the impression that you don't have to do anything; just lie back, relax, and enjoy God's blessing.

"Just name it and claim it," they often proclaim.

"Let go and let God!"

"Start believing and acting like the promise is already yours, and it will be."

There is a measure of truth in all of these teachings, but there is also a biblical balance between the two extremes. I call that harmonious position *positive holiness*. Understanding that our holiness depends upon God and is derived from God, we can then say that God expects us to do our part, as well. He will do His 100 percent, but He expects you to do your 100 percent.

Scripture says to pursue holiness (Hebrews 12:14), with the idea being "to diligently go after it; to expend whatever effort is necessary, no matter how long it takes, or what it costs." This is your personal obligation and responsibility.

God will not do for you that which He expects you to

do for Him. He will supply the power you need, but He still expects *you* to do it. For example, Scripture says, "Therefore, having these promises, beloved, let us cleanse ourselves from all defilement of flesh and spirit, perfecting holiness in the fear of God" (2 Corinthians 7:1). Notice, that in this instance, the burden of responsibility is upon you. The implication is that by drawing upon God's power, you *can* put away that sin, that attitude, or that evil habit that has been mastering you. But you need to make up your mind, once and for all, that you are going to do it. Stop playing spiritual games. Quit blaming everyone else and acknowledge your own responsibility in the matter.

Some Christians spend most of their time asking God to do what He has already commanded them to do! One fellow had been praying for years that God would deliver him from his cigarette addiction. Every time he was in prayer with other believers, he would pray, "Oh God, please deliver me from these filthy cigarettes!" After hearing him pray this way for several years, a sweet, diminutive woman finally grew tired of his failure to experience victory over his smoking habit. Following a church service one night, she approached him. "I've been praying with you about your cigarette habit for some time now," she began. "Are you still having trouble?"

"Oh! Yes, Ma'am, I am!"

"Then throw the filthy things down and don't ever pick them up again!" she told him bluntly.

At first, he almost became offended at the woman's words. But then he realized that God had been speaking to him for a prolonged period of time, and her words were only a confirmation of a message that he had been trying to ignore for too long. He took her advice to heart, threw out his cigarettes, and has not smoked since.

Certainly we are dependent upon the Holy Spirit's power to deliver us. We can do nothing apart from Him. In that respect, it is quite true that "our faith overcomes the world." Yet at the same time, spiritual victory is a by-product of spiritual obedience. As you obey the commands of Jesus, and live daily under the control of His Spirit, you will enjoy victory over sin. Holiness is the way to victory; spiritual victory is the result of holiness.

Jerry Bridges reminds us,

> Our reliance on the Spirit is not intended to foster an attitude of "I can't do it," but one of "I can do it through Him who strengthens me." The Christian should never complain of want of ability and power. If we sin, it is because we choose to sin, not because we lack the ability to say no to temptation. . . , It is time for us Christians to face up to our responsibility for holiness. Too often we say we are "defeated" by this or that sin. No, we are not defeated; we are simply disobedient![3]

The life of holiness is similar to an oil lantern: If you keep the glass clean, the fire inside can be seen and it will give off light and warmth to everyone around. But if you allow the glass of the lantern to get encrusted with filth and crud and grime, even though there is a light inside, the lantern will be practically useless.

Maybe Jesus had that in mind when He said, "Let your light shine before men in such a way that they may see your good works, and glorify your Father who is in heaven" (Matthew 5:16). In other words, keep the glass clean and shining, and the light will stream through to those in darkness.

How can you "keep your glass clean"? Here are three simple principles:

1. Keep short accounts with God. In other words, when
   the Holy Spirit convicts your heart and mind of sin and
   you realize that something is wrong, when you know
   that you have thought, said, or done something dis-
   pleasing to God, be quick to confess that sin. Immediately!
2. Seek God's forgiveness and cleansing; repent, and turn
   away from that sin.
3. Own up to your responsibility and make right what
   was wrong. If this involves restitution, do so insofar as
   you are able.

If you will do these things, then you can live a consistently clean, holy, Christian life. Understand it is God's
will that you be holy! An unholy Christian is a contradiction of terms! If a farmer plants a field of potatoes, he
expects a harvest of potatoes, not corn! If that same farmer
plants corn, he expects a harvest of corn, not potatoes. And
if Jesus Christ is real in our hearts, it only makes sense
that we should expect to see Christ-like characteristics
cropping up in our lives! If not, you have every right to
wonder if Jesus Christ is planted in you, if you have ever
truly trusted Him as your Savior and Lord.

God's Grading System

Sometimes, even those who do understand that sin is
an offense against God's holy character still give the
impression that God grades on a curve. They live as
though some sins are okay for Christians. They would
agree that certain sins are totally unacceptable, but would
also feel that others are tolerable.

The Bible says it is "the little foxes that spoil the vines"
(Song of Solomon 2:15 KJV). Those little areas of compromise will be your undoing. You might say, "Aw, it's not

so bad! Everybody else is doing it." Watch out! This is one of the devil's most devious devices and if you do not turn around and begin moving in the correct direction, you will continue the downhill slide toward destruction.

Please understand: It is not the magnitude of the law that was broken that is so important. But it is the majesty and the holiness of the Lawgiver that matters! Jesus is our standard by which we are to live, and He is the standard by which we will be judged! We need to take sin seriously, not because a particular sin is "big" or "little," but because our holy God hates it, forbids it, and gave His Son, Jesus, to deliver us from it. Dr. Daniel Yutze, a sociology professor at Taylor University, is fond of saying, "There is no such thing as a little sin, because there is no 'little' God to sin against!"

Let's try an experiment. Please list in the space below those sins which are permissible for God's people to commit. Go ahead—write them down. Then you can quit worrying about them!

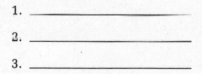

1. _____

2. _____

3. _____

You will notice that the publisher wisely did not leave you much space. That's a hint. The Apostle John gives you another clue: "My little children, I am writing these things to you that you may not sin . . ." (1 John 2:1). He continues later in his letter by straightforwardly declaring, "The one who practices sin is of the devil. . . . The Son of God appeared for this purpose, that He might destroy the works of the devil. No one who is born of God practices sin, because His seed abides in him; and he cannot sin, because he is born of God" (3:8, 9).

The key phrase here is "practices sin." John is not saying that it is *impossible* for a Christian to sin. He is stating, however, that it is absolutely inconceivable for a Christian to continue in habitual, deliberate sin and remain in close relationship with Christ.

Therefore, if you want to be holy, your first step should be to deal radically with willful, deliberate sin and to repent of it. God will not allow you to get away with anything less.

You need to settle these issues in your heart right now. Today, right this moment, will you begin to look at sin as an offense toward God and not simply as a personality defect? Will you begin to take responsibility for your sin, to confess it and allow the blood of Jesus to cleanse you? Will you decide to obey God in every area of your life, no matter how big or how small, no matter how seemingly insignificant? If so, you will take a major step toward positive holiness.

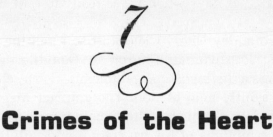

Crimes of the Heart

Many years ago, Henry Clay Morrison pastored the First Methodist Church in Danville, Kentucky. Mr. Morrison quickly earned a reputation as a brilliant young preacher, extremely capable both as a scholar and as an orator. He had no problem producing eloquent sermons, but he did have trouble practicing what he preached. As Morrison became more acutely aware of the difference between his Sunday morning messages and the manner in which he lived the remainder of the week, he became deeply uncomfortable with the gross discrepancies. His concern over his spiritual "heart condition" increased until it grew to a great and agonizing soul cry that God would remedy his internal conflict.

He later said, "There were days when I thought I would

die, and other days when I was ready to quit the ministry."

Then one day Henry Clay Morrison met the pastor of
the First Presbyterian Church in Danville. The older
pastor was a distinguished gentleman, also a scholar, and
a wise, saintly man of God. The younger Mr. Morrison
began to pour out his heart to the older minister, describing the symptoms of his frustration and failure in great
detail. Finally, he asked, "Sir, what is wrong with me?"

The older pastor looked at Henry and answered kindly,
"Mr. Morrison, God is preparing you for something you
have not known. We Presbyterians call this 'the deeper
life.' Some people call it the 'life of faith.' Others refer to
it as 'the way of surrender.' But John Wesley, your patron,
called it 'Perfect Love,' or 'Entire Sanctification.' That is
what God is preparing you for, and this will be what
makes the difference in your ministry."

That Presbyterian pastor probably did not know it at
the time, but his words were prophetic. God *did* do
something within the heart of Henry Clay Morrison that
transformed him from an extraordinarily gifted preacher
into one of the flaming spiritual leaders of his day. He led
him into holiness. What God did in the life of that young
preacher He is equally willing to do in your life. He may
not make you into a preacher, but you can be sure He will
make you into an effective servant and representative of
Him.

If you study Church history carefully, you will quickly
discover that great Christians throughout the years have
described some experience subsequent to their salvation
whereby they entered into a deeper relationship with
Christ. The terms they used to describe this experience
vary widely, but if you distill and discern the common
denominators of their experience, you will discover that

they were talking about a life of holiness, a life that is surrendered to and controlled by the Holy Spirit.

Nor are their testimonies restricted to individuals of similar theological persuasions, nationalities, race, sex, or life-style. Men and women as disparate as Hudson Taylor, A. B. Simpson, Andrew Murray, Dwight L. Moody, Harold John Ockenga, Phoebe Palmer, Oswald Chambers, Amy Carmichael, Blaise Pascal, Charles Finney, Corrie ten Boom, A. J. Gordon, John Bunyan, Ian Thomas, and a host of others all bear witness to an experience that took place at some point *after* their salvation, an experience that totally revolutionized their *Christian* lives as much or, in some cases, more so than their conversion had transformed them.

In the introduction to his book *They Found the Secret*, Raymond Edman, former president and chancellor of Wheaton College, wrote concerning these enigmatic saints, "The pattern of their experiences is much the same. They had believed on the Savior, yet they were burdened and bewildered, unfaithful and unfruitful, always yearning for a better way and never achieving by their efforts a better life."

Does that sound at all familiar to you? If so, you will be glad to know that such ignominious darkness and defeat also once characterized the lives of Christianity's most valiant heroes. Yet something happened to change them. What made the difference in their lives?

Dr. Edman continues,

They came to a crisis of utter heart surrender to the Savior, a meeting with Him in the innermost depths of their spirit; and they found the Holy Spirit to be an unfailing fountain of life and refreshment. Thereafter life was never again the same. . . .

Out of discouragement and defeat they have come into
victory. Out of weakness and weariness they have been
made strong. Out of ineffectiveness and apparent useless-
ness they have become efficient and enthusiastic.

The pattern seems to be: self-centeredness, self-effort,
increasing inner dissatisfaction and outer discouragement, a temptation to give it all up because there is not a
better way; and then finding the Spirit of God to be their
strength, their guide, their confidence and companion—in
a word, their life.[1]

None other than the premier patriarch of "positive
thinking" himself, Dr. Norman Vincent Peale traces his
success to an experience such as this. It was during the
depths of the worst economic depression the United
States has ever known that Dr. Peale found himself the
victim of discouragement and disillusionment. Though
he continued to preach to others concerning the positive
power of faith in Christ, he himself was running on
empty, his life a stretched-out rubber band, tension-filled,
stressful, and close to snapping.

He and his wife, Ruth, decided they needed a vacation,
so they traveled to the Lake District of England and
booked a room at the Station Hotel in Keswick. While
they were there, they underwent what Dr. Peale later
referred to as "the supreme spiritual experience of our
lives."

Said Dr. Peale:

We tried to relax and enjoy ourselves, and Ruth was
able to accomplish that quite successfully . . . but I was
disconsolate, low in spirit, plagued by self-doubt. . . . The
gloom of New York and the desolate state of the church
had pervasively seeped into my mind and discolored it.

Despite my enthusiastic preaching back in New York, I was myself pretty low on optimism.

The hotel was situated in a magnificent English garden with clipped hedgerows and formal flower beds and well-placed benches from which you could look out at the glorious hills roundabout. We walked daily in this garden and in particular sat on one bench at the far end. There I would pour my woes into the ears of my loving and patient young wife.

But one day as we were seated together on that bench she said, "Norman, you are my husband, but you are also my pastor. I sit in church and listen to you preach the gospel of Christ with love and enthusiasm. But to hear you talk now, I wonder if you actually have any faith at all . . . . What you need to do," she continued, "is to surrender your church, your problems, your entire self to Christ. You have done this before, but do it again now, and perhaps even in greater depth. As you do this, I promise you will receive peace, joy, new energy, and a quality of enthusiasm that will never run down. . . ."[2]

In desperation, Dr. Peale prayed a simple but genuine prayer. He describes his experience as follows:

"Dear Lord Jesus," I prayed, "I cannot handle my life. I need help. I need You. I hereby with all my heart surrender my mind, my soul, my life to You. Use me as You will. Fill me with Your Holy Spirit." We sat together hand in hand. Then it happened; such peace as I would never have dreamed possible surged through me, and with it a burst of joy. It was like light, like glory. Suddenly every dark, gloomy shadow in my mind fled and a light, like the most radiant morning took the place of those old dark things, sweeping them out as with a huge broom.

I was elated. I leaped to my feet and began to pace up and down. "It's wonderful!" I declared. "It's wonderful!

Praise God! I love Jesus Christ, I love everybody, I love
you," and I swept her into a fervent embrace. . . .
    I can tell you in complete sincerity that from that
moment life was never again the same. Ruth's promise
proved a fact. I received an enthusiasm that has never run
down. And that peace has remained. The dear Lord has
been my Friend all the way. This was the greatest spiritual
experience of my life.[3]

It is interesting to study how such personal experiences
have impacted the efforts of evangelism and social
change. Unquestionably, this emphasis upon total surrender and a deeper work of the Lord Jesus in the heart of the
believer was a keynote with John Wesley, the founder of
Methodism. Wesley was one of the Church's most effective evangelists and is generally credited with being used
by God to stir the great spiritual revival in England which
subsequently prevented that country from falling to the
same social frustration that precipitated the disorder and
devastation of the French Revolution.
    Why was Wesley so successful? One person who sought
and found the answer to that question was the outstanding English preacher William Sangster. Sangster had the
largest Sunday evening congregation in London during
World War II, filling the 2,500 seats in Westminster's
Central Hall. He was not content, however, to see scores
of people respond to his evangelistic preaching; he was
more concerned about the permanent spiritual fruit such
efforts brought forth. Consequently, he did a study, after
which he said, "I came to the conclusion that there are
many evangelists whose works are very temporal and
transient. You can come back a few years later, and there
will be little trace of any permanent fruit. On other

occasions, there is fruit that seems to last and gets brighter as the years pass by."

Sangster discovered that the spiritual fruit from John Wesley's ministry was of the latter, lasting sort. After further studying Wesley and his work, Sangster found one of the main reasons for the evangelist's eternal effectiveness: When a person came to new faith in Jesus Christ, Wesley immediately set in front of him or her a higher goal to be attained. Sangster realized that to Wesley, salvation was not a terminal experience, whereby a person could say, "Now I am in." Rather, to Wesley, conversion was the initial step, the point at which a person could say, "Yes, now I have begun; now which way should I go? How should I now live?" Wesley would then set in front of his converts the goal of personal holiness—the day-to-day ideal of inner love and sanctity which would result in his or her character taking on the attributes that were evident in the earthly life of the Lord Jesus.

Wesley was not dangling spiritual carrots out in front of his converts in order to keep them coming along spiritually. He was not trifling with them as if to say, "Aha! You thought you had it, but you really don't!" On the contrary, he never minimized a person's salvation experience. He was merely saying, "Now that you are saved, there's something more." W. E. Sangster concluded that it was this emphasis upon the "something more" that set Wesley's work apart from most other evangelists of his time.

Wesley's approach was quite similar to the Apostle Paul's thrust in his first letter to the young Christians at Thessalonica. Paul had not known these "baby believers" for long when he penned these heartfelt words:

For indeed when we were with you, we kept telling you in advance that we were going to suffer affliction; and so it

*came to pass, as you know. For this reason, when I could
endure it no longer, I also sent to find out about your faith,
for fear that the tempter might have tempted you, and our
labor should be in vain. But now that Timothy has come
to us from you, and has brought us good news of your
faith and love, and that you always think kindly of us,
longing to see us just as we also long to see you, for this
reason, brethren, in all our distress and affliction we were
comforted about you through your faith; for now we really
live, if you stand firm in the Lord. For what thanks can we
render to God for you in return for all the joy with which
we rejoice before our God on your account, as we night
and day keep praying most earnestly that we may see
your face, and may complete what is lacking in your
faith? . . . may the Lord cause you to increase and abound
in love for one another, and for all men, just as we also do
for you; so that He may establish your hearts unblamable
in holiness before our God and Father at the coming of
our Lord Jesus with all His saints.*

1 Thessalonians 3:4–10, 12, 13

Paul was obviously concerned for the spiritual health
of these new Christians. He had only taught them for
three weeks when he and Silas had gone through Asia
Minor on the Apostle's second missionary journey.

As soon as Paul arrived in Thessalonica, he went to the
Jewish synagogue to preach. It was the missionary's
normal method of operation to take the Gospel message to
the Jews first, fervently preaching to them that Jesus is the
Messiah. This he did on three successive Sabbaths (Acts
17:2), "explaining and giving evidence that the Christ had
to suffer and rise again from the dead, and saying, 'This
Jesus whom I am proclaiming to you is the Christ' "
(17:3).

Some of the Jews in Thessalonica believed Paul's message; so did a great many God-fearing Greeks, as well as many of the leading women of that city. Others of the Jews did not believe, however, and along with some of the wicked men from the marketplace, they formed an angry mob intent upon silencing Paul and his friends once and for all. They stormed the home of Jason, searching for Paul. But Paul was not there; he had already been smuggled out of the city. Irate, the unbelieving Jews hauled Jason and some of the new Thessalonian Christians before the authorities and exacted a pledge from them that there would be no further trouble.

Meanwhile, Paul and his friends scurried south to the community of Berea, where the message of Christ was eagerly received. Before long though, the unbelieving Thessalonian Jews found that the word of God had been proclaimed in Berea. The rabble-rousers raced southward and began agitating and stirring up the crowds in Berea, too.

Once again, the Apostle was sent packing. Paul and friends fled to Athens, where the missionary's concern for his new converts began to break his heart. From Athens, he went on to Corinth, but Paul sent Timothy back to search out the situation in Thessalonica.

When Timothy returned to Paul, he brought back a glowing report of the Thessalonians' faith and love, and how they were standing strong even in the face of intense difficulties and persecutions.

No wonder when Paul wrote to the Thessalonians, he wrote with such a fond, approving, fatherly tone. Nevertheless, he was concerned for them. He wanted to instruct them about that "something more." He wanted to complete that which was lacking in their faith. Paul was rejoicing over their certain salvation, delighted about the clear-cut testimony they had maintained, and he was thrilled that their faith was growing stronger in the midst of trouble.

Yet, he said, there's more, much more! His prayerful concern for the Thessalonians was that their hearts would overflow with supernatural, superabounding love, and that the Lord would establish their hearts "unblamable in holiness" (1 Thessalonians 3:12, 13).

If the Apostle could board a time capsule and streak through the years until he arrived at the waning moments of the twentieth century, undoubtedly his prayer for the Christian church in your town and in mine would be similar to his heart-cry for the new believers in Thessalonica. "Can't you see," he would implore, "there is more! Much more is possible in this Christian life than what you are currently experiencing. I want you to be able to stand strong against persecutions; I want you to be so firmly established that the transitory temptations that Satan throws at you cannot shake you or cause you to stumble. I want our hearts to overflow with holy, pure love for one another, and for God, and for a world that is dying without Jesus. I want you to be *ready* when Christ returns, to be clean, to have hearts that are unblamable in holiness at His second coming!"

A Time for Truth

Is it possible to live a Christian life and miss Paul's point? Unfortunately, it certainly is.

Praise '87 was the name of a renewal emphasis held during the summer of 1987 at Pierce Memorial Church in Rochester, New York, which included the faculty, staff, and students from Roberts Wesleyan College. At this gathering, a profound visitation of God took place when one of the most popular preachers in North America publicly admitted to his need for holiness.

The night before he was scheduled to speak at Praise '87, John Wesley White picked up the local newspaper, "The Rochester Democrat Chronicle," and was suddenly struck by a headline summarizing the sex and avarice scandals that rocked the Christian Church in 1987. The words that stood out from the article and seared into the heart and mind of John Wesley White were, "Where Has Holiness Gone?"

If anyone should have been able to answer that question, it was John Wesley White. Dr. White had preached in over one hundred countries; he had written nineteen books and had received degrees from Moody Bible Institute, Wheaton College, and Oxford University. He had served as an associate evangelist with the Billy Graham Evangelistic Association for many years and was world-renowned as an articulate spokesman for Jesus Christ.

Nevertheless, the events of the spring and summer of 1987 had broken the evangelist's heart and had rekindled a desire within him for personal holiness, as well as for corporate purity within the Body of Christ. Consequently the next morning, White began haltingly by saying, "I am only here because of two celebrated names, Billy Graham and John Wesley, whose name I bear unworthily. I have not had the luxury of being brought up and nurtured in the holiness movement but. . . .

"If there is kind of an ancient lady here, who combs her hair straight, and isn't wearing any jewelry at all, or makeup, and perhaps her skirt is as long as my daughter-in-law's wedding garment, someone like that has a lot to say to me and to all of us in this conference as we hearken back to the origins of this great movement.

He continued:

> To my shame, and I say it apologetically, I have never
> before looked in the Scriptures in depth at that word
> holiness. And I've never gone through my concordance
> and looked up holy. And it's never been a theme for a
> sermon that I've preached in the forty-three years that I
> have been in the ministry. But the last twenty-four hours,
> and since five A.M. this morning, I've been poring over the
> words holiness and holy. And I want to announce at
> the outset, this morning, what the Lord has laid on my
> heart.
>
> I have seen tens of thousands of people respond to Billy
> Graham Crusade invitations to come to Christ. I want to
> do something I have never done in my life before, and I do
> it with extreme sensitivity and reluctance. I'm going to be
> the first one forward this morning, God willing. I want to
> come down and stand, not as a counselor, but as an
> inquirer, as a searcher, as a seeker, here at this altar.
>
> And if there is a little old lady about eighty-five years of
> age, like I have already described, who has had a very
> special experience of sanctification, or holiness, or what it
> was called in John Wesley's day, the baptism with the
> Holy Ghost, I am going to come down and stand here in
> the front and maybe you would come and stand by me.
>
> Dr. Paul Rees, perhaps the most articulate evangelical in
> this generation here in the United States, coming out of a
> holiness movement, the Swedish Covenant Church, has
> stated, "Holiness is a crisis that proceeds to a process"
> and this morning it's my prayer that that experience, that
> crisis, might occur in my life, in many of our lives, as we
> assemble at this altar this morning.

John Wesley White then went on to preach his first
sermon ever on the subject of holiness. At the close of the
message, Dr. White reiterated his plea, "If there is a little

old lady, with no makeup and no rings, and a big long skirt, and she wants to come down and stand by me and pray for me, that would be like an angel from heaven." He then invited others in the auditorium whose hearts were hungry for holiness to join him at the front of the sanctuary. He left the platform and led the way among a host of seekers. There, Dr. John Wesley White and hundreds of others prayed that God would cleanse their hearts and fill them with His Holy Spirit.

The need that Dr. White sensed had nothing to do with rings, or makeup, or long skirts. But in asking for such a prayer warrior to intercede for him, the evangelist was crying out for someone who knew the holiness of God and understood what it meant to walk in purity before a holy God. Although it went against his theology, was contrary to much of his education, and had never concerned him throughout a lifetime of preaching, the need of his heart, he finally realized, was for cleansing and for the filling with the Holy Spirit.

Undoubtedly, John Wesley White is not the only Christian who had never previously considered the matter of holiness. At a private meeting, one well-known Christian leader lamented recently, "Before we can evangelize the lost, we must face the extremely low level of sanctity among our own ranks. Even in positions of leadership within the Church, we are finding little difference between the life-styles and attitudes of the Christian and the non-Christian. What we really need is a revival of holiness among our believers. Then, we can have the effective witness to the non-Christian world that we ought to have."

Perhaps that is one reason why the Apostle Paul spelled out holiness in relationship to sexual purity. To the Thessalonians, he wrote, "For this is the will of God, your sanctification; that is, that you abstain from sexual immorality" (1 Thessalonians 4:3). He went on to tell the Thessalonians that God had called them to holiness, not impurity (4:7).

Paul, a master at making such vivid juxtapositions of incongruous elements is here contrasting the highest ideals of Christian living with the lowest, most common, profanations of the pagan world. He was saying to the Thessalonians and to us that, as Christians, we are not to live under the tyrannical influence of "lustful passion, like the Gentiles who do not know God" (1 Thessalonians 4:5), but rather, we are to live under the control and dominance of the Holy Spirit, who will motivate us to the highest, most positive levels of Christian living.

Obviously, a fleeting glance at either secular society or Christian conclaves will quickly remind you of the relevance of Paul's exhortations for believers nineteen centuries later. Thankfully, the remedy remains the same, as well.

Dr. Dennis Kinlaw, president of Asbury College, relates the story of a young man who, although he desired to live for Christ, continually found himself stepping back into the sin of sexual immorality. Finally, the fellow went into the woods and cried out, "Oh, God! There's no point in all of this unless You can do more in me than You've already done. I can't live, if I have to live in this kind of defeat!"

The young man had been a sporadic student of the Bible, but he knew little theology or Church history, and he was totally unprepared for the answer to his prayer. Suddenly, God came to his heart in such a mighty demonstration of His presence and His power that it seemed to the young fellow that the whole earth shook.

He raced out of the woods and continued running all

the way home. There, he encountered his brother and breathlessly inquired, "Are you okay?"

"Okay?" his brother answered with a quizzical expression on his face. "Sure, I'm okay. Why wouldn't I be?"

"Because the earth quaked! Didn't you feel it?"

"Earthquake? There hasn't been any earthquake. Are you crazy? Have you been drinking or something?"

"Oh, yes, there *was* an earthquake," the young man shouted. "I *felt* it!"

"No," his brother replied calmly, "Not in these parts, anyhow."

Later, the young man realized that he had not felt the earth quaking; it was his heart that was *breaking*, breaking wide open with the cleansing power of God. As the Holy Spirit cleansed the fellow of his addiction to lust, He was filling him with His supernatural power of pure, holy love.

"Since then," the young man said, "the Lord has given me the power to live in the Spirit, rather than in the flesh."

This is what Paul so longed for the Thessalonian Christians to experience. Since he could not yet return to them personally, he wrote specific instructions for these new believers, fleshing out the skeleton of their rudimentary faith in Christ. Paul reminded them that they were called to *love*, and not simply to love selfishly the way the world does; they were called to ". . . increase and abound in love for one another, and for all men . . ." (1 Thessalonians 3:12). They were to live for *others* first, in stark contrast to the "Me-ism" all around them.

They were also called to live *expectantly*. Throughout his letter to the Thessalonians, Paul frequently refers to the return of the Lord Jesus Christ for those who love Him and are living in close relationship to Him.

To Paul, this was a great incentive toward holy living. He taught the Thessalonians to expect Jesus to physically return for them at any moment (1 Thessalonians 4:13–18) and even described some of the details about His return that had raised questions in some of the Thessalonians' thoughts. Then he said, "Therefore comfort one another with these words" (4:18). Obviously, your heart better be pure if you are to be comforted by the thought that at any moment, Jesus might appear!

Paul also encouraged these excited Christians to allow their lives to be characterized by respect for authority, joy, prayerfulness, and thanksgiving. Paul told them that they should "rejoice always" (1 Thessalonians 5:16); to "pray without ceasing" (5:17); to give thanks in *everything*, in every circumstance of life (5:18); and to live without quenching the Holy Spirit (5:19). They were to examine everything, but to hold fast only to that which is good; and they were to abstain from every form of evil (5:21, 22). All of this they were to do in the face of intense and prolonged persecution.

Paul described to the Thessalonians how a life of holiness is to be lived:

- Your life is to be one of positive, practical purity rather than fleshliness, self-indulgence, and sin.
- It is to be love and self-giving, rather than selfish, egocentric love and an emphasis upon *getting*.
- It is to be lived with an orientation toward the return of Christ, and with an attitude of joy at the prospect of His Second Coming, as opposed to becoming possessively "sticky-fingered" and consumed with success here on earth during this lifetime.
- It is to be doing good to all of those around you, so nobody can truthfully speak evil about you.
- It is a life characterized by joy, prayer, and thankfulness.

"Is that really possible?" you might ask.

No. Not humanly. Not under your own willpower or good intentions. But it is possible to live in such a positive, holy manner when the Spirit of God empowers you from within. Paul intimated this to the Thessalonians when he concluded his letter to them, "Faithful is He who calls you, and He also will bring it to pass" (1 Thessalonians 5:24).

One of the most shocking best-sellers to hit the bookstands of America in recent years was Armando Valladares' *Against All Hope*. The book is Valladares' stunning account of life inside one of Fidel Castro's prisons. At twenty-three years of age, Armando, a devout Christian who dared to oppose communism, was dragged from his home in the middle of the night, arrested, handcuffed, and cast into one of Castro's hellholes for the next twenty-two years of his life. In the midst of unimaginable horrors, there was one man who inspired Valledares and others to endure. They called him the "Brother of Faith."

One day, the thousands of prisoners "corralled by rifles and bayonets" were herded in from the forced-labor fields. Valledares recalls,

They were dirty, some of them barefoot and others with their clothing hanging from them in tatters. Their backs and shoulders were bowed and bent as though they carried all the weight of bitterness and human misery in the world on their shoulders. The muddy roads . . . were full of the long columns of men winding to their cells from another wearying day's work in mosquito-infested swamps, in quarries, in the fields of citrus trees our blood fertilized. . . .

The prisoners, undernourished and bent with fatigue, could only trudge heavily, slowly. . . . Then the guards would unleash a hail of bayonet or truncheon blows over

the heads of the men at the front of the lines, and the file
of men would move a little faster. . . . They didn't walk,
they dragged themselves. They hardly had the strength to
lift their feet. The guards yelled at them to speed it up and
threatened them with machetes and bayonets. The prisoners made an effort, but the escorts wanted even more,
and they began to beat them. . . . The blows of the machetes and the bayonets on the prisoners' backs sounded
like low thunder. The file began to break up, but the
guards chased the men down, striking out blindly. . . .

Suddenly one prisoner, as the guards rained blows on
his back, raised his arms and face to the sky and shouted,
"Forgive them, Lord, for they know not what they do!"
There was not a trace of pain, not a tremble in his voice;
it was as though it were not his back the machete was
lashing, over and over again, shredding his skin. The
brilliant eyes of the "Brother of Faith" seemed to burn; his
arms open to the sky seemed to draw down pardon for his
executioners. He was at that instant an incredible, supernatural, marvelous man. His hat fell off his head and the
wind ruffled his white hair. Very few men knew his real
name, but they knew that he was an inexhaustible store of
faith. He managed somehow to transmit that faith to his
companions, even in the hardest, most desparate circumstances.[4]

Valladares recounted that the prisoners lived in constant fear of Castro's firing squads, but when one of their
brave companions met death by a bullet,

the Brother of Faith would say that the prisoner they
had shot was a privileged man, that God had called him to
His side.

He helped many men face death with strength and
serenity. He came and went constantly among the groups

of men, trying to instill faith, trying to calm their spirits, trying to give support.

When they opened the *galeras*, he would go through them, looking for sick men, and whether the sick men wanted him to or not, he would carry off their dirty clothes. And you would see him down there in the prison yard, with a piece of burlap bag or plastic tied around his waist like an apron, standing over mountains of dirty clothes, bent over the wash-basins with sweat pouring off him. . . .

If some exhausted or sick prisoner fell behind in the furrows or hadn't piled up the amount of rock he had been ordered to break, the Brother of Faith would turn up. He was thin and wiry, with incredible stamina for physical labor. He would catch the other man up in his work, save him from brutal beatings. When one of the guards would walk up behind him and hit him, the Brother of Faith would spring erect, look into the guard's eyes, and say to him, "May God pardon you". . . .

His constant labor was to teach us not to hate; all his sermons carried that message.[5]

What God did in the lives of Henry Clay Morrison, Norman Vincent Peale, John Wesley White, and the Brother of Faith, He can and will do in you, if you will allow Him.

That, my friend, is positive holiness.

Beauty and the Beast

I spend most of my life dressed up, either in a business suit and tie or dressy casuals. Sometimes, though, it's fun just to be sloppy, to go into my office in an old sweatshirt with cutoff sleeves, and wearing a pair of beat-up blue jeans with holes in the knees. Some of my musician friends dress that way every day, lucky souls, but because of my varied responsibilities, it is usually inappropriate for me to appear at the office without "proper" attire. Except on Saturdays. Saturdays are my "messies' days."

One messies' day, I was at my best, or worst, depending upon how you regard being unshaven, unkempt, and dressed in the grubbiest of grubby clothes. With letters and messages that needed attention overflowing my desk, papers strewn in a semicircle around my chair, books cluttering my couch, three coffee cups—two of which were half full—positioned at strategic locations around the room for easy access, my Bible and four notebooks lying open in front of me, the dictaphone purring beside me, ready to record my next utterance, and an open box of graham crackers perched atop the telephone, I thought I was in "Messies' heaven."

What a wonderful work environment! I mused. I was loving it and diligently pursuing a new project, oblivious to almost everything around me, when suddenly I heard the front door open and somebody walking down the corridor, unannounced and uninvited. Quickly, I bounded out from behind my jumbled desk and flung open my office door.

There he was—Mr. Perfect. He stood silently shocked, with his arm raised and knuckles frozen in midair, ready to knock on my inner office door. "H-hi, Ken!" he blurted out before I could say anything. "I was just in the neighborhood, so I thought I'd drop by to see you."

Mr. Perfect was the president of an important company in Pittsburgh, and we had enjoyed a scheduled appointment at my office a few months prior to his surprise visit. His previous stop had been on a weekday, a day when the office complex was bustling with busy people, and, of course, I was dressed appropriately.

Now, here he was on a messies' day. Only he was still perfect—perfectly dressed in an expensive, stylish suit, every hair neatly in place, cleanly shaven, shoes smartly shined, briefcase in hand, and looking every inch the sophisticated chief executive officer that he is. He was Mr. Perfect; I was Mr. Messie.

Funny . . . as long as I was doing my own thing, and was not in the presence of perfection, I was quite content with my condition, totally unconcerned about the chaos all around me. I was comfortable amidst the crud.

When Mr. Perfect walked in, immediately I was cognizant of my own uncleanness and the mess surrounding me. In comparison to his perfect appearance, my rumpled grubbies suddenly began to itch and crawl on my body. I became instantly aware that my hair was mussed and tangled and that my face was rough and unshaven. I darted a quick glance at my desk and the deluge of debris looked dreadful. Graham cracker crumbs that a few moments earlier had gone unnoticed now appeared gigantic in the presence of Mr. Perfect. The dismal disorder on open display all around me suddenly became a hideous embarrassment to me in front of Mr. Perfect. I had no comprehension of how filthy and foul I had allowed myself to become until I was confronted with perfection.

Something similar to that is going to happen on Judgment Day. The moment men and women are confronted with Jesus Christ, the One who truly *is* Mr. Perfect, they will be immediately impressed by His majesty; at the same time, they will be overcome at the awfulness of the muck and muddle of their own lives in comparison to Him. Millions of people who previously said, "Well, my conscience doesn't bother me; I guess I must be okay" will suddenly be stricken with a sense of inadequacy and guilt such as they have never known before, when they stand in the presence of He who is holy.

Perhaps that is why the Apostle Paul's prayer for the Christians at Thessalonica was: "Now may the God of peace Himself sanctify you entirely; and may your spirit and soul and body be preserved complete, without blame at the coming of our Lord Jesus Christ" (1 Thessalonians 5:23).

This magnificent prayer could easily stand alone as a beautiful piece of prose. Nevertheless, you get the distinct impression that Paul is not simply spouting pious-sounding platitudes; he really meant this prayer. What's even more astounding is that he obviously intended to imply that it is possible for the specifics of this prayer to be realized in *this* life, not in heaven to come. He says you are to be holy *now*, to be unblamable *before* Jesus returns to earth, so you will not be embarrassed but will be able to meet Him with joy and confidence. Paul does not say that you should simply be working toward holiness, He says you are to be holy—and not just partially holy, but entirely holy, or you could say, *wholly* holy! Furthermore, the blamelessness for which he prays on behalf of the Thessalonians is not to be an occasional holiness, lasting for only a few minutes following the preacher's sermon. Paul says that you are to live this way until the Lord Jesus comes again.

Unquestionably, Paul is writing this word to believers. In fact, the Thessalonians were functioning extremely well in their new faith. Granted, genuine holiness is attractive even to a nonbeliever, but it remains a curious enigma, and little more. When a person has truly come to know Jesus Christ, however, he or she immediately begins to sense a desire for holiness. Although they may not know what to call it, they intuitively begin to sense their need in this area. The closer a believer gets to Jesus, the more he or she wants to be like Him.

If you claim to know Christ and have little or no desire for holiness, or you are not seeking to be more like Him, it may be a clear indication that you have never really met Him. You may have become religious. Maybe you have changed a few matters of your conduct; you may have even joined a church. Still—and I say it with love and concern, not as a word of condemnation—if you have no desire for holiness, you would be extremely wise to examine yourself to see if you are truly in the faith (2 Corinthians 13:5). Something about our relationship with Jesus creates within even the worst of us a desire to be holy as He is holy.

It is always *distance* from Christ that lulls you asleep in the light. The further away from His holiness that you get, the more likely you are to tolerate willful compromise and sin in your life. You probably well remember the account of Peter denying the Lord three times the night that Jesus was arrested. But have you ever noticed where Peter's denial began? Both Mark and Luke poignantly point out that Peter was following Jesus *"at a distance"* (Mark 14:54; Luke 22:54). Dr. Luke, a physician with a keen eye for detail, put it this way: "And having arrested Him, they led Him away, and brought Him to the house of the high priest; but Peter was following at a distance. And after they had kindled a fire in the middle of the courtyard and had sat down together, Peter was sitting among them" (Luke 22:54, 55).

Peter *sat down* at a time when perhaps he should have been standing up for Christ. He sat *among them*. Among whom? Among the friends of Jesus? Among the other disciples of Christ? No, he sat down among the enemies of the Lord, the scoffers, the accusers, the revilers, and the servants of the very high priest who had been scheming for weeks how he could have Jesus killed!

It is always dangerous to attempt to follow Jesus from a distance. The downward progression is inevitable: distance, compromise, denial, sin. As a believer, the closer you come to Jesus, the safer and more secure you are.

For the unbeliever, the exact opposite is often true. The closer the non-Christian gets to Jesus and His holiness, the more uncomfortable he or she becomes. They recognize that He is different, and they realize that *they* are fundamentally different from Him. When an unbeliever confronts Christ, the Holy Spirit begins to convict that person of "sin, and righteousness, and judgment" (John 16:8). If, at that point, the person does not respond positively to His holiness, he or she will want to escape from His presence as soon as possible.

You can easily see this in the attitudes and conduct of the Pharisees during Jesus' day. They were enamored with Jesus, yet they were repelled by Him at the same time.

One day the scribes and the Pharisees hauled in a woman who was actually caught in the act of adultery (John 8:3–11). The punishment for such an offense according to Jewish Law was death by stoning, and the religious leaders who brought her before Jesus knew that. Have you ever wondered why they would bother to bring such a woman to Jesus? To test Him, certainly (8:6), but maybe there was an ulterior motive behind their actions.

Perhaps what troubled those malicious men the most, subconsciously at least, was the fact that they could never get around Jesus for long without becoming extremely sensitized to, and disconsolate about, their own sin. Something about being in the presence of Jesus disturbed them. In the face of absolute holiness and goodness, they found themselves irresistibly wanting to flee from Him.

No doubt, this must have puzzled the scribes, and especially bothered the Pharisees. After all, the one thing that every good Pharisee prided himself upon was the fact that he was morally superior to most ordinary men. Yet every time they got near to this carpenter's kid from Nazareth, they discovered to their dismay that He made them feel guilty and unclean. How shocking it must have been for those men who lived most of their adult lives with a "holier-than-thou" attitude to suddenly encounter

Someone whose very presence seared their consciences with an inescapable awareness of their own sinfulness.

No wonder, when they found a woman caught in the act of adultery, an unmistakably major moral misdeed, the devious thought crossed their sin-darkened minds, *Let's take her to Jesus! Surely, compared to her, we must look pretty good.* They may have thought, *Certainly we will be comfortable in His presence when He compares us with this woman whose obvious moral failures cause us to stand in righteous, bold relief.*

But Jesus wasn't playing by their rules. When they approached Him with their trick question, He simply stooped down and began writing in the dirt with His finger (John 8:6). Some scholars have suggested that Jesus was writing the names of the men in that group who had also had immoral, adulterous affairs. Possibly so, but the Bible doesn't say. One thing for certain, when He said to them, "He who is without sin among you, let him be the first to throw a stone at her" (8:7), He sent the scribes and Pharisees scurrying for cover. When the powerful spotlight of the Holy Spirit turned upon their hearts, those proud, pious, self-righteous scribes and Pharisees slipped away as rapidly as possible from the presence of He who is holy.

The Closer You Get

Strangely, this consciousness of guilt over sin does not diminish when you are converted to Christ. On the contrary, the closer you get to Jesus, the more self-conscious you become about your sins. Before you met the Lord, even the "big sins" hardly bothered you; now, the small, seemingly insignificant sins cause you to be seriously concerned about your spiritual state.

This creates an unusual paradox: Whereas in your life before knowing Christ, something about the holiness of Jesus struck fear into your heart and caused you to want to flee from His face; now, if you truly know Him, you find His holiness to be irresistibly attractive. Yes, you still have a fear of God, but it is no longer the fear of an outlaw on the run, or the fear of a cowering child awaiting punishment for disobedience. Now, your attitude toward your heavenly Father is one of reverential awe.

You long to be with Him and to remain in His presence for prolonged periods of time. You desire to draw closer to Christ, but you have a problem. You know that He cannot stand sin, and yet, if there is anything of which you are certain about yourself, it is that you are sinful. Your sinfulness makes you want to cry out in shame and despair. This dilemma has driven many devout Christians to destruction. It nearly killed Martin Luther.

Martin Luther is probably best known as the "Father of the Protestant Reformation." Most scholars mark the moment Luther tacked his famous ninety-five points for discussion on the Castle Church door in Wittenberg, Germany, as the beginning of the movement that changed the course of history. For Luther, however, the Reformation had begun much earlier.

As a devout Catholic monk, he had diligently attempted to do anything necessary to obtain peace with God. He studied the Scriptures and prayed for hours on end. Often he would spend six hours or more in the confessional, confessing his most picayune imperfections, foibles, and character flaws. He had taken a much-revered pilgrimage to Rome, where in an act of contrition, he had climbed the Vatican steps on his knees, pausing on each step to pray. Still, his soul was unsatisfied.

If any man could ever have become holy by mere

human effort and merit, Martin Luther probably would have made it. But Luther finally realized that no matter what he did, or how obediently he performed the rites of the Church, he remained stuck in a quagmire of sin.

Luther was not an insane masochist. Quite the contrary: Luther was brilliant. He was especially astute in the field of law. It was his grasp of legal matters that caused Luther to comprehend that a holy Judge could not compromise His integrity in order to exonerate unholy sinners like himself.

R. C. Sproul, in *The Holiness of God*, accurately sums up Luther's problem when he writes:

> The genius of Luther ran up against a legal dilemma that he could not solve. There seemed to be no solution possible. The question that nagged him day and night was how a just God could accept an unjust man. He knew that his eternal destiny rode on the answer. But he could not find the answer. Lesser minds went merrily along their way enjoying the ignorance of bliss. They were satisfied to think that God would compromise His own excellence and let them into heaven. After all, heaven would not be the marvelous place it was cracked up to be if they were excluded from it. God must grade on a curve. Boys will be boys, and God is big enough not to get all excited about a few moral blemishes.
>
> Two things separated Luther from the rest of men: First, he knew who God was. Second, he understood the demands of the Law of that God. He had mastered the Law. Unless he came to understand the gospel, he would die in torment.[1]

Fortunately for Luther, and for us, he discovered the phrase in Paul's letter to the Romans, "the just shall live by faith" (Romans 1:17 KJV). Luther was intrigued. What did it mean?

In describing his feelings, Luther later said,

> Night and day I pondered until I saw the connection between the justice of God and the statement that "the just shall live by his faith." Then I grasped that the justice of God is that righteousness by which through grace and sheer mercy God justifies us through faith. Thereupon I felt myself to be reborn and to have gone through open doors into paradise. The whole of Scripture took on a new meaning, and whereas before the "justice of God" had filled me with hate, now it became to me inexpressibly sweet in greater love. This passage of Paul became to me a gate to heaven.[2]

When Luther came to these conclusions, he had no idea of the volatile power of his words or the explosive events that would ensue. He was not attempting to instigate a church rebellion when he tacked his ninety-five theses on the door; he just wanted to debate the issues. Nevertheless, to defend his freshly discovered doctrine of salvation by faith, Luther had to stand against an entire Church that had long since slid into legalism.

Basically, Luther asked the bold question, "What is required for a person to be saved, what is *essential* to salvation?" His answer spawned a reformation of the Catholic Church and the birth of the Protestant churches that flourish today. Luther's conclusion that faith alone—trusting in Jesus Christ—rather than works, was all that is necessary to be saved, has lost some of its radical flavor for modern believers who have accepted it as fact for more than four hundred years. It got Luther excommunicated and almost killed.

Nearly two centuries later, John Wesley and a host of

other holiness teachers began to build upon Luther's foundations. They said, "Yes, thanks to Brother Martin, our eyes have been opened; we now know what it takes to be saved. But can God do something even *more* in our lives?"

It is important for us to understand this difference. Luther was not primarily concerned with holiness. Although his legal mind grappled with God's demanding justice, Luther was engrossed in how he could find forgiveness and freedom from his sins. The question that predominately occupied the minds of Wesley and other holiness advocates was, "Now that I am saved, how can I bring my life into conformity with what God wants?"

Luther's emphasis was upon "Christian liberty;" Wesley's was upon "perfect love." Luther and his followers asked, "What can I still do and remain a Christian?" Wesley and his followers asked, "How can I bring my life to the place where it is an expression of pure, perfect love for Christ and for others?" There lies the fundamental difference between the thinking of Luther and Wesley. Unfortunately, many theologians have attempted to pit the doctrines of these two heroes against each other, as if they were in opposition. In fact, it is not an "either/or" choice. A person who positively desires to please Christ should incorporate *both* truths into his or her life-style.

Historically, Wesley came *after* Luther; perhaps that is a providential paradigm, illustrating the pattern of concern that will appear in your life. *After* you come to know Christ and what it means to be saved, you will want to know how you are to live and love in a manner pleasing to Him. This subsequent seeking for holiness may seem as intense and as fraught with frustration as your search for salvation, and maybe more so.

This should not surprise you. Every great Christian has

had to pass this way on his or her journey through the stages of spiritual growth. The wise founder of the Christian and Missionary Alliance Church, A. B. Simpson, wrote, "As we get farther on in our Christian life, God will hold us much more closely to obedience in things that seem insignificant."[3]

Unquestionably, that is why the more intimate and mature you desire your relationship with Jesus to be, the more aware you will become of not merely your sins, but also your *sinfulness*—that attitude or condition within you that *wants* to sin. You discover that sin has seeped more deeply into your heart than you realized, and the problem now is not just that you commit sinful acts or hold onto sinful attitudes. The problem is that there is a *nature* within you that automatically tends to produce evil thoughts, dirty deeds, awful words, and atrocious attitudes.

The Road Less Traveled

At this point, you are at the fork in the road. One of two things usually happens in the life of a Christian, when he or she gets here. One, you may grow accustomed to sin in your life, take the easy road, and most likely sputter and stall in your spiritual journey. If you choose this option, the consequence will be a cold, hard, callous relationship to Christ. Moreover, you will soon find yourself becoming increasingly argumentative at home with your family and with your colleagues at work or school. You will find yourself experiencing a sense of intense frustration and failure in your personal relationships; you will be contentious toward other Christians, jealous, miserable, and generally, not a lot of fun to live with! You may respond as did one successful young businessman who went this

route and later said, "Secular society told me all that I
needed to do was to *find* myself. Well, I found myself . . .
and the person I found was a real creep!"

Understand, if you choose the second option, you are
not signing up for an easy trip, but you will truly be
pursuing "the road less traveled," the route the greatest
saints of the past and present have trod. It is the path
toward personal holiness. As you start down this road,
one of the first obstacles you will encounter will be your
own innate sinfulness.

One of the most famous experiences of this sort was
that of Hudson Taylor, the founder of the China Inland
Mission, a fabulously effective, interdenominational and
international faith mission work.

Hudson Taylor was a young Englishman who, at the
age of seventeen, committed his life to Jesus Christ. Not
long after that, God led him to become a missionary. At
age twenty-one, he set sail for China. There he poured out
his life on the mission field. A few years after he had been
ministering in China, a financial crisis arose within the
mission society. In order to continue serving in China,
Hudson Taylor resigned from the mission board and
became an independent missionary. He was virtually on
his own, with no financial support except for what God
providentially supplied for Him. Taylor's motto was
"Jehovah Jirah—The Lord will provide."

He was a great pioneer. Radically committed to Jesus,
he was also a missions innovator who dressed in the
clothes of the Chinese people. His conviction was that he
had not gone to the mission field to convert the Chinese to
English culture; he went to convert them to Christ. And
he did!

Strangely, it was after being on the mission field for
more than fifteen years that he came to the place in his

life where he could not stand his own sinfulness any longer. It was not his conduct that concerned him; it was his unclean heart. He had undergone terrible difficulties for Christ. He had endured physical and spiritual struggles. He had proven himself to be unflinchingly solid in his commitment to the Lord. Nevertheless, one day this dedicated missionary sat down and wrote in a heart-rending letter to his mother: "I have often asked you to remember me in prayer, and when I have done so, there has been much need of it. That need has never been greater than at present."

Obviously, Hudson Taylor was having difficulties. You can sense his despair and depression. He continued, "[I've been] envied by some, despised by many, hated by others, often blamed for things I never heard of or had nothing to do with, an innovator on what have become established rules of missionary practice, an opponent of mighty systems of heathen error and superstition, working without precedent in many respects, and with few experienced helpers, often sick in body as well as perplexed in mind, and embarrassed by circumstances. . . ."[4]

Despite his trials, he wrote, "Had not the Lord been specially gracious to me, had not my mind been sustained by the conviction that the work is His and that He is with me in what it is no empty figure to call 'the thick of the conflict' I must have fainted or broken down. But the battle is the Lord's, and He will conquer. We may fail—do fail continually—but He never fails. Still, I need your prayers more than ever."[5]

Now, follow closely how Hudson Taylor described his spiritual condition. Remember, the man who wrote this was one of the most dedicated missionaries in his day; a man who was in the thick of the battle for the Lord, a man who ventured all for Jesus Christ. Still he wrote:

But I have continually to mourn that I follow at such a distance and learn so slowly to imitate my precious Master. I cannot tell you how I am buffeted sometimes by temptation. I never knew how bad a heart I have. Yet I do know that I love God and love His work, and desire to serve Him only and in all things. And I value above all else that precious Saviour in whom alone I can be accepted. Often, I am tempted to think that one so full of sin cannot be a child of God at all.[6]

Notice, he was writing about his *sin*, not about his sinful acts. Hudson Taylor knew that isolated sinful actions could be repented of and forgiven. But here Taylor was concerned about the sinful condition of his heart. He continued to describe the battle in which he found himself:

But I try to throw it back, and rejoice all the more in the preciousness of Jesus and in the riches of the grace that made us "accepted in the beloved." Beloved He *is* of God; beloved, He ought to be of us. But oh, how short I fall here again! May God help me to love Him more and serve Him better. Do pray for me. Pray that the Lord will keep me from sin, will sanctify me wholly, will use me more largely in his service.[7]

Here was a man who was widely respected and deeply loved by evangelical Christians of his day. A great man. A godly man. Yet he was crying out, not because of his sins, but because of his sinfulness.

It is a simple spiritual principle: The closer you get to Jesus, the more you see how holy He is and how sinful you are. If you are sensitive to His Spirit, your heart cries out, "Oh, God! Can't you do something more in me than you have already done? Won't You please cleanse me of myself?" Of course, the answer is a resounding "Yes!" to both questions; He can and He will cleanse you that thoroughly, if you will allow Him to do so.

Earlier, I mentioned that Henry Clay Morrison experienced something similar to this. At a time when Morrison was a highly effective and extremely popular pastor and evangelist, he realized, "My heart was in my work, but there was uncleanness in my heart!" He said, "I had lurking within me a volcano of evil temper which would leap into a consuming flame in a moment if I thought anyone proposed to trample upon what I thought were sacred, personal rights."

Obviously, for Morrison, one way this inherent sinful nature manifested itself was through his temper, or what the Bible refers to as "outbursts of anger" (Galatians 5:20). The temper lurked within him, a temper of volcanic proportions, just waiting to be triggered. Any incursion into what he considered to be his sacred, personal rights could cause an explosion.

Morrison is not alone. Sadly, many Christians have lost their testimonies to the world and their peace with God because of inconsistencies in their tempers.

A preacher once held a citywide crusade and was greatly used of the Lord to get people saved and bring spiritual revival to that town. Then he went to the next town, where he was to preach outdoors in a tent. While he and a group of men were pitching the tent, somebody angered the preacher and he lost his temper. With that one outburst, he destroyed the effectiveness he had enjoyed in other places.

The people who saw and heard his lapse into carnality could not receive his words from the pulpit until he had repented and made things right with those he had offended. More critical for him personally, he had broken his peace with God and had grieved the Holy Spirit.

Something similar often occurs at church board meetings, or during other types of ministry meetings, or backstage at Christian music concerts, at home, in your classroom at school, in your office at work, or out on the ball field.

Somebody blows his or her stack. Then after tempers cool down, everyone pretends that life is back to business as usual. But it's not. Repentance is required! Apologies are in order. The Spirit of God has been grieved or possibly quenched. Prayer for forgiveness and a refilling of the Holy Spirit, and then restitution should be the top priorities before anything else is undertaken. Otherwise, you will go right back to the spiritual fork in the road I mentioned earlier and will have to start over.

Broken Vessels

Another way that inherent sinfulness is often displayed is through self-will. This is the attitude that says, "I want what I want."

All of us are naturally intent upon having our own way. If you are like most people, you probably spend the majority of your time, energy, resources, money, and influence trying to get your own way. Yet, one of the things you will notice repeatedly throughout Scripture and in biographies of great Christians is this: There are no holy men or women who have not been broken somewhere. Inevitably, you will discover that their self-will had to be broken before they could effectively do God's will.

For example, when God met with Jacob at Peniel, He touched Jacob's thigh and Jacob limped away. Think about that! It is quite possible that Jacob walked with a limp for the rest of his life. If so, do you see the irony? The man God chose to use as a blessing to the world had to live with a God-inflicted limp in the midst of a society where a person who was crippled was considered to be accursed! It made no sense to the world. Undoubtedly that leg caused Jacob several sleepless nights, too. Nevertheless, when Jacob was broken, it was the turning point in his life with God.

You'll find something similar in the lives of most of the individuals who are, or have been, godly people down through history. If you look closely, you will find that mark of brokenness, where their wills were broken so God could have His way in their lives, and so He could bless them and make them a blessing to others. Sometimes they had to accept a cup that they may not have wanted or would not have chosen if there had been any other way. But when they accepted it and allowed God to have His way, they discovered that it was not the way of death, but it was the way of life. Abundant life!

In one spiritually dry church, they were having trouble finding Sunday school teachers. One lady, however, seemed to have an interest and a bit of talent in that area. The only problem was that the woman held some rather unorthodox doctrines. She believed in God, but not in Jesus or the Holy Spirit. Still, the pastor desperately needed teachers, and he figured that believing in One out of the Three was better than no faith at all, so he asked her to teach. As she studied for her class, she came into contact with the Scriptures. The Holy Spirit spoke to her, illumined her mind, and she met Jesus Christ! She was wonderfully converted and became a godly woman. Suddenly, the biblical data came alive to her and she began to teach out of her own personal experience with Christ and what the Holy Spirit was instructing her.

Can you guess what happened? Folks at that dead church got upset. They found her exuberance offensive. Her friends resented her and called her names like "Holy Roller" and "Church Lady." After all, they had been attending this church for years; some of them had even helped to establish it and had worked with their own hands to help raise up the building.

Angrily, they lashed out, "We were here long before she ever showed up! We were doing fine without her, and we certainly don't need her to tell us what is right or wrong. Maybe *she* needs all that born-again stuff, but we are just fine the way we are!"

Heartlessly, the leaders of the opposition circulated a petition throughout the church, asking the congregation to remove the woman from her position as one of the Sunday school teachers. She was the best teacher in the church, and she was the *only* teacher who genuinely knew God! But they threw her out.

The preacher heard about what had happened so he went to visit her. As soon as they started talking about the situation, she began to weep. She said, "You know, I've searched all my life for spiritual reality, and just when I've finally found it. . . now this happens! I guess I will have to leave the church!"

The preacher asked, "Why would you do that?"

Through her tears, the woman replied, "Well, I can't go back where they don't want me!"

"That's exactly what you must do," the pastor answered.

"You wouldn't expect me to go back into a church where they have circulated a petition to get rid of me, would you?"

The preacher hesitated for a moment, and then softly responded, "Well, they crucified Jesus. When He came, they didn't want Him either. But these people need Christ and you know Him! You can't leave now. And you certainly can't leave under these circumstances."

"What about my husband?" she cried.

The woman's husband was not a Christian. He was a huge, burly man, one of the roughest, toughest fellows you would ever want to meet. He held most "church people" in disdain. In fact, he had threatened concerning one of the leading churchmen in town, "If he says another word to me, I'm going to mop up the streets with him!" No one who knew him doubted his ability or his will to do it.

The woman continued her lament, "Preacher, my husband has heard about this mess, and he wants to take everybody at that church apart—limb by limb! So you know I can't go back to that church with him."

"You have to," the pastor answered flatly.

Wide-eyed, she replied, "You mean you want me to walk back into that church, sit down in that Sunday school class, and listen while somebody else teaches in my place, in my class?"

"Yes. But don't go unless you can go without feeling judgmental in your heart and mind. Don't do it if you are going to go with a Pharisaical attitude." The preacher then pressed her further. Quietly but firmly, he asked, "Can you go and sit there and lovingly pray for the person who takes your place?"

"You can't ask me to do that!"

"No, I can't. But I believe Jesus is asking you to do that."

The preacher left and the woman spent the rest of the day weeping and wondering what she should do. Finally, she got down on her knees beside her bed and gave the matter to the Lord.

The next Sunday, she was at church. She was broken. She had reached the point where what she *wanted* was no longer important.

Before stepping into the sanctuary, she prayed, "It doesn't make any sense to me, but even if it is a cup of bitterness, I will take it, if that is what You want me to do, Lord. Have Your way with me." Then, in brokenness and humility, she went and attended her class.

A few weeks later, a distraught man was waiting for the preacher at the church. He had a look of absolute horror on his face.

Nervously, he blurted out, "Pastor, have you heard about Mrs. ———'s husband?"

The preacher's first reaction was to think, *"Oh no! He must have died, or worse yet, maybe he killed someone else!"*

Attempting to maintain his calm demeanor, the pastor took a deep breath before answering. "No, I haven't heard anything. What are you talking about?" he replied, as he braced himself to hear the bad news.

The fellow said, "Well, he says that he found Christ last night!"

"What?" the preacher responded dumbfoundedly. "What are you talking about? Where is he?"

"He's at home I think," answered the parishioner, "clothed and in his right mind!"

The pastor hurried to the home of the former Sunday school teacher and found her husband. One look at the man's countenance told the preacher that something significant had taken place. "Man, what happened to you?" he asked pensively.

The husband laughed and said, "Oh! Preacher! Last night I found Jesus Christ!"

The pastor cried, "You what? How did you do that? We didn't even have church last night! There aren't any revivals going on around here anywhere!"

The husband looked back at the preacher and spoke quietly, "No, but for the past few weeks, I've been living with one that wears skirts."

He said, "I've watched my wife go in and kneel down by her bed every night and pray. You know, I never went for that stuff. Then this church problem came up, and I told her, 'You just let me go up there! I'll straighten out every one of those church people!'

"She said, 'No. No; it's okay.' "

He said, "I listened to her pray. Every night, she prayed lovingly for every one of those people who had hurt her so deeply. Till finally, I couldn't take it anymore. I said, 'Stop it! Don't pray for them. Quit praying for those people . . . Would you please pray for me? They don't need it as much as I do. Pray for me.' And last night, by our bed, she led me to Jesus Christ."

Granted, that is not normal twentieth-century Christianity, is it? But it is quite normal biblical Christianity. It is the place where God wants us to live on a regular, day-to-day basis.

He wants to bring you to the place of brokenness, where you can say, "Have Thine own way Lord. Cleanse me of self and my sinfulness, so thoroughly and completely that I am free to be your vessel, a vessel of honor, that You can fill and can use for Your glory."

Do you need a cleansing such as that? In your relationship to your husband? wife? roommate? kids? parents? boyfriend, girlfriend, or boss? Has somebody done something to you that you don't like? Consequently, you sense some attitudes in yourself that you don't like. Jesus sees them, too, and He wants to deliver you from that bondage. You need to be cleansed and filled with His perfect love.

You might ask, "What can I do about it?"

That's the sticky part. You can't do a thing to solve this problem—except to surrender to Him, to trust Him, and to allow Jesus to be Lord in your life. That's why Paul told the Thessalonians, "Faithful is He who calls you, and He also will bring it to pass" (1 Thessalonians 5:24).

There is nobody else who can, but if you believe Him in sheer faith, He is capable. He is able to cleanse your heart so thoroughly that you can pray sincerely, "Not my will, but Thine be done."

That innate depravity can be dealt such a death blow by the Spirit of Christ that you will no longer have to live under the domination of sin. Yes, you will be broken. But you will also be holy, positively holy.

Incentives to Holiness

You don't hear much about heaven these days. You probably hear even less about hell, unless someone is encouraging someone else to go there. Which is rather strange, when you stop to think about it, since nearly every major survey in the past thirty years reveals that few people actually *believe* in a literal hell anymore. Many modern clergymen no longer subscribe to the idea of a place of eternal punishment.

A few years ago, a popular rock star offered his rather dubious observations on the subjects of heaven and hell. He declared, "I know there is no heaven, and I pray there is no hell." Apparently, he missed the irony of his own statement.

One man, to whom I was attempting to explain the Gospel, emphatically told me that hell kept him out of church.

"No sir," he said, "I don't like to go to church and hear all that preachin' about hellfire and brimstone." Obviously, he had not been to church in a long, long time. Most contemporary preachers rarely speak about hell; some have never publicly broached the subject. Many congregations simply don't want to hear about it.

Yet the Bible is replete with references pungently depicting a place of eternal punishment known as hell. If you are a verse counter, the sheer volume of biblical data is overwhelming. Scripture has nearly three times as much to say about God's justice, judgment, wrath, and punishment of sin than it does the love and mercy of God. But then, who's counting?

Four different words were translated "hell" in the King James Version of the Bible. The word for "hell" used most frequently in the Old Testament is *sheol,* a shadowy underworld, or a place of the dead. Nothing is said about fire and brimstone, but Sheol is not exactly the kind of place where you would enjoy spending eternity.

In the New Testament, the word *hades* carries much the same meaning as Sheol. Another word, *tartarus,* is used only once by the Apostle Peter to describe the place where disobedient angels were sent when they sinned (2 Peter 2:4).

The most frequently used word for hell in the New Testament is *gehenna.* Ten of the eleven times it is recorded, it comes from the mouth of Jesus Himself. (The other instance is in James 3:6 and refers to the destructive capabilities of a person's tongue.) *Gehenna* means "a final place of punishment for the ungodly."

Originally the word referred to the valley of Hinnom, located just outside Jerusalem. During the evil reigns of the kings Ahaz and Manasseh, the valley was notorious as the place where human sacrifices were offered to the heathen god Molech. By the time of Christ, it had become the garbage dump of Jerusalem. Because of the potential for disease and infestation from the refuse, the garbage was set ablaze. Still the maggots, worms, rodents, and other vermin were abundant. Keeping the health hazard under control was a constant battle. It seemed that the stench, squalor, fire, and smoke were a perpetual part of life in the valley of Hinnom.

No wonder when Jesus wanted to describe the horrors of hell in human terms, He used the word gehenna. He called it a place of everlasting punishment; a place of outer, absolute darkness. Seven times in the Gospels, He referred to hell as a place where people are weeping and gnashing their teeth. He called it a furnace of fire, a place prepared for the devil and his angels, and perhaps with the garbage dump in mind, Jesus said it is a place where the worm never dies and the fire is not quenched. It is the garbage dump of human history.

This creates a problem for those who insist upon perceiving Jesus as a mellow, "I wouldn't hurt a fly" type of God. Some people naively say, "I believe in Jesus, but I don't believe in hell." What they fail to realize is that most of the information we have about hell comes not from fire-breathing prophets or apostles; it comes from the mouth of the Meek and Gentle One, Jesus Himself.

It was Jesus who said, ". . . whoever shall say to his brother, 'Raca,' shall be guilty before the supreme court; and whoever shall say, 'You fool,' shall be guilty enough to go into the hell of fire" (Matthew 5:22). It was Christ who rebuked the disciples for fearing what mere men could do to them: "And do not fear those who kill the body, but are unable to kill the soul; but rather fear Him who is able to destroy both soul and body in hell" (10:28).

Near the end of His earthly ministry, Jesus delivered a long discourse to His disciples, discussing His Second Coming. In describing the King's judgment upon hypocritical, self-centered, uncaring disciples, He said, "Then He will also say to those on His left, 'Depart from Me, accursed ones, into the eternal fire which has been prepared for the devil and his angels' " (Matthew 25:41).

In the Apostle John's futuristic view of the Revelation of Jesus Christ, hell remains just as horrible. John writes, "And death and Hades were thrown into the lake of fire. This is the second death, the lake of fire. And if anyone's name was not found written in the book of life, he was thrown into the lake of fire" (Revelation 20:14, 15).

Christ warned that hell is a place to be avoided at all costs! He said, "And if your right eye makes you stumble, tear it out, and throw it from you; for it is better for you that one of the parts of your body perish, than for your whole body to be thrown into hell" (Matthew 5:29). Whether Jesus' words are to be interpreted literally or figuratively, there is no escaping the thrust of their content. Clearly, Jesus took the matter of hell quite seriously. Men and women who hope to walk with Him must do the same.

First, you should do everything—anything—necessary to avoid the horrors of hell yourself, living cleanly before your God in holiness. Second, if you have a heart for God, you must be concerned enough over the eternal destinies of your fellow men that you are willing to do anything necessary to see them saved from the fires of hell. It is inconsistent, not to mention a mockery of your holy God, for a Christian to be unconcerned about the souls of men and women for whom Christ died. To be a Christian means to be Christ-like; Christ was concerned enough to go all the way to a cross. He gave His life for you. Now, He

expects you to give up your life for Him and for the
burdens that "break the heart of God." That's why hell is
an incentive to holiness.

Perhaps if contemporary Christians could grasp even
an inkling of that concept, it would be a tremendous
stimulant toward holy living and having compassionate
concern for those who are hurting and helplessly dying
without Christ. Besides causing you to nurture and guard
your own soul, the reality of men and women spending
eternity in hell should motivate your concern for evangelism and missions. It certainly did for Charlie Studd,
whose inspiring story is told in C. T. Studd by Norman
Grubb.

"C. T." Studd acquired a bright sense of business
acumen and possessed a keen enough mind that he
probably could have entered most any profession and
been a success. He chose, however, to pour out his life in
China and Africa as a missionary. The vision of lost souls
entering into a hellish eternal existence gripped his
heart and caused him to eschew any material success he
could have pursued. He said, "How could I spend the
best years of my life in working for myself and for the
honours and pleasures of this world, while thousands
and thousands of souls are perishing every day without
having heard of Christ?"[1]

Shortly thereafter, C. T. heard about the possibility of
being filled with the Holy Spirit, the potential for peace in
the midst of perplexity, and the importance of living in
holiness if a person is to be an effective servant of Christ.
It all started when a friend asked him, "Have you heard of
the extraordinary blessing Mrs. W. has received?"

"No," Studd answered.

"Well, you know she has been an earnest Christian
worker nearly her whole life, and she has had a good deal

of sorrow and trouble, which has naturally influenced and weighed upon her. But lately somehow God has given her such a blessing that it does not affect her at all now. Nothing, in fact, seems to trouble her. She lives a life of perfect peace. Her life is like one of heaven upon earth."[2]

Studd was intrigued. He said, "We began at once looking into the Bible to see if God had promised such a blessing as this, and it was not long before we found that God had promised it to believers, a peace which passeth all understanding, and a joy that is unspeakable. We then began to examine ourselves earnestly, and we found that we had not received this. But we wanted the best thing that God could give us, so we knelt down and asked Him to give us this blessing. Then we separated."[3]

C. T. Studd did not drop the matter. He continued,

I was very much in earnest about it, so when I went up to my own room I again asked God to give me this peace and joy. That very day I met with the book *The Christian's Secret of a Happy Life*. In it was stated that this blessing is exactly what God gives to everyone who is ready and willing to receive it. I found that the reason I had not received it was just this, that I had not made room for it, and I found . . . that I had been keeping back from God what belonged to Him. I found that I had been bought with the price of the precious blood of the Lord Jesus, and that I had kept back myself from Him, and had not wholly yielded.

As soon as I found this out, I went down on my knees and gave myself up to God in the words of Frances Ridley Havergal's Consecration Hymn:

> *Take my life and let it be,*
> *Consecrated, Lord, to thee.*

I found the next step was to have simple, childlike faith, to believe that what I had committed to God, He was also willing to take and keep . . . From that time my life has been different, and He has given me that peace that passeth understanding and that joy which is unspeakable.[4]

Shortly after that, C. T. Studd left for the mission field in China. His burden for souls had led him to seek a holy heart, and then his holy heart compelled him to be concerned for lost souls. His life was not one of ease, nor was it without opposition from friends and foes alike. Neither was he immune from life's infirmities. But the passion of his life was to tell lost men and women how they could find Jesus.

His dedication and devotion to Christ and concern for souls did not diminish with time, but instead grew stronger. One day in 1908, when C. T. was already fifty years of age, his body wrecked and weakened by sickness, he was walking down the street when suddenly a poster caught his attention. The poster read: "CANNIBALS WANT MISSIONARIES!"

"Hmmm. That's odd," thought Studd as he drew closer to find out more information. He discovered that the poster was advertising a speaker, Dr. Karl Kumm, a famous explorer of Africa. Studd decided to attend. What he heard once again seared his holy heart with concern for lost souls.

He later wrote, "Dr. Kumm said there were numbers of tribes who had never heard the story of Jesus Christ. . . . Explorers had been to those regions, and big-game hunters, Arabs and traders, European officials and scientists, but no Christian had ever gone to tell of Jesus.

"The shame sank into one's soul," said Studd. "Why

have no Christians gone?" he asked to himself as much as to God. He was unprepared for the Lord's reply.

"Why don't you go?" God asked him.

C. T. quickly recalled his poor physical health and answered honestly, "The doctors won't permit it."

God responded, "Am I not the Good Physician?"

Less than two years later, C. T. Studd, as surprised as anyone, set sail for Africa. Literally thousands of Africans were won to Jesus Christ through his efforts before he died in 1931; and World Evangelism Crusade, the great organization he spawned, continues to spread the Gospel to this day.

Heavenly Hope

If hell is an incentive to holiness (although admittedly a somewhat negative inspiration), the possibility of living eternally in *heaven* should positively motivate us toward holy, Christ-like lives! The writer to the Hebrews recognized this connection. He said, "Pursue peace with all men, and the sanctification [holiness] without which no one will see the Lord" (Hebrews 12:14). This verse is a bit confusing, and has been variously interpreted, but the obvious, unalterable truth cannot be ignored: A clear prerequisite to future intimate fellowship with the Lord is holiness here and now. As such, heaven should motivate us toward holiness, and holiness is the avenue by which we travel toward heaven; access to both being made possible only by the blood of Jesus Christ.

While many Christians and non-Christians alike cannot comprehend the concept of hell, heaven can be even more enigmatic. Where is it? What does it look like? Why don't the astronauts bump into it in outer space? Good questions.

Preachers used to warn people about being so heavenly-minded that they were no earthly good. You probably haven't heard that reminder much lately. Nowadays, most Christians are so wrapped up in and attached to this world, few ever think, talk, or seriously contemplate eternity. Until the earth quakes.

Nevertheless, the Bible states quite a bit about heaven. The subject is mentioned fifty-two times in the Book of Revelation alone! Hundreds of other references to heaven are sprinkled throughout Scripture.

Granted, when the Bible speaks of heaven, the writers were not always describing eternal bliss. Many times the term is used to describe the atmospheric conditions and the skies above us. Jesus sometimes used the phrase "Kingdom of Heaven" synonymously with His spiritual Kingdom (Matthew 5:3, 10:7; 16:19). But the Bible also pictures a place called heaven, which is the abode of God.

This is where the Christian's true citizenship lies, the Apostle Paul tells us (Philippians 3:20). This is where Christ resides currently, seated at the right hand of God. Paul says, therefore, as one of His saints, you should "Set your mind on the things above, not on the things that are on earth. For you have died and your life is hidden with Christ in God. When Christ, who is our life, is revealed, then you also will be revealed with Him in glory" (Colossians 3:2–4). Here, Paul again is indicating the clear interrelationship between heaven and holiness, which he describes as "a life hidden with Christ." Heaven is an incentive to holiness and heaven is also the reward for holiness.

What do we know about heaven and why should we want to go there?

First and foremost, we know that heaven is the home of Jesus. Certainly, His Spirit lives within the hearts of all true believers. But in heaven, you will see Jesus, alive and in person! When the Messiah is manifested a second time, every person who ever lived will see Him—even those who crucified Him. Quoting the prophets Daniel and Zechariah, the Apostle John wrote, "Behold, He is coming with the clouds, and every eye will see Him, even those who pierced Him . . ." (Revelation 1:7).

What an astounding thought! You are going to see the Holy One! A friend of mine had a personal audience with the Pope, and that person's life has never been the same. Another friend was received by England's royal family, and at the reception, he could barely eat, because his stomach was fluttering so badly. Can you imagine being in the presence of the King of kings, the One who is absolutely holy?

You will be there—guaranteed. And you won't be late. You may be the world's worst procrastinator, but this is one appearance you will not put off; this is one meeting you will not miss. You may avoid Jesus Christ all of your life on earth. You may attempt to shut Him out of your life, by ignoring or rejecting His presence, but the one Person you can count on meeting some day is Jesus. It will be the ultimate encounter of your life.

On that day, if you know Him and have been pursuing a life of holiness, He will welcome you into your heavenly home. If you do not know Him and have not been living a life of holiness, you will hear Him utter the words that will haunt you throughout eternity in hell: "Depart from Me, you who practice lawlessness" (Matthew 7:23).

Not only is heaven the home of the Holy One, Jesus promised that it would be the eventual and eternal dwelling place of all His holy ones, the saints. The night before His crucifixion, Jesus told His disciples, "I go to prepare a place for you. And if I go and prepare a place for you, I will come again, and receive you to Myself; that where I am, there you may be also" (John 14:2, 3). Can your mind conceive of the kind of place that the regnant, all-powerful King is creating for those whom He loves?

John attempted to describe heaven (sometimes referred to as the "New Jerusalem" or the "holy city") as a huge cube, approximately fifteen hundred miles in each direction (Revelation 21:16). The predominant building material of the holy city seems to be pure gold (21:18). The New Jerusalem has walls of jasper (21:18), and has twelve gates, three entrances on each side (21:21). An unusual river is there, "a river of the water of life, clear as crystal, coming from the throne of God and of the Lamb, in the middle of its street. And on either side of the river was the tree of life . . ." (22:1, 2).

Of course, it is difficult to determine how much of John's vision is to be interpreted literally and how much should be interpreted symbolically, but there is no question that he is picturing a magnificently gorgeous place.

What will you do there? Billy Graham has often stated that he believes at least part of our time in heaven will be spent working. Probably so, but the Bible doesn't really say. It does indicate that in heaven we will have complete and unrestricted fellowship with our holy God. John reveals, "And I heard a loud voice from the throne, saying, 'Behold, the tabernacle of God is among men, and He shall dwell among them, and they shall be His people, and God Himself shall be among them . . .' " (Revelation 21:3).

One of the paramount and most exciting activities of heaven will be entering into a previously unexperienced dimension of true praise and worship of the Lord. We will join the four living creatures of Revelation 4:8 who "do not cease to say, 'Holy, holy, holy, is the Lord God,

the Almighty, who was and who is and who is to come' "
(Revelation 4:8).

Undoubtedly, we will sing along with heaven's
twenty-four elders who "will fall down before Him who
sits on the throne, and will worship Him who lives
forever and ever, and will cast their crowns before the
throne, saying, 'Worthy art thou, our Lord and our God to
receive glory and honor and power; for Thou didst create
all things, and because of Thy will they existed, and were
created' " (Revelation 4:10, 11).

John was given a glimpse of our heavenly future and he
grappled for words to describe it: "And I looked, and I
heard the voice of many angels around the throne and the
living creatures and the elders; and the number of them
was myriads of myriads, and thousands of thousands,
saying with a loud voice, 'Worthy is the Lamb that was
slain to receive power and riches and wisdom and might
and honor and glory and blessing.'

"And every created thing which is in heaven and on
the earth and under the earth and on the sea, and all
things in them, I heard saying, 'To Him who sits on the
throne, and to the Lamb, be blessing and honor and glory
and dominion forever and ever' " (Revelation 5:11–13).

Apparently, praise is going to be the predominating
language of heaven. Worship will no longer be "worked
up" but will flow naturally from the hearts of holy
people to the heart of their holy God.

It is interesting to note what will *not* be in heaven.
There will be *no sea* (Revelation 21:1), which leads some
scholars to speculate that there will be no more separation
of loved ones.

No *tears* are in heaven, either. Nor is there any *death*,
mourning, *crying*, or *pain* (Revelation 21:4). Neither will
there be any *temple* (21:22); no *sun*, no *moon* (21:23); no

night, no closing of the gates (21:25); nothing unclean, or we could say, nothing unholy (21:27). The curse of sin will have been broken (22:3) and Jesus will be Lord indeed!

Certainly, a heaven such as this should motivate you toward holiness. Why? Because heaven is a holy place. Everything about heaven is holy. The Lord of heaven is holy. The angels and the other creatures who are worshiping the Lord Jesus are holy. The redeemed saints of God are holy. Everything and everyone in heaven is holy!

This causes the truth of Hebrews 12:14 to loom much larger: Without holiness, no one shall see the Lord. It implies that if you are a stranger to holiness now, what in heaven would you do? Without being holy here on earth, it is highly doubtful that you will be ready for heaven or even able to enjoy it.

Consider this: Suppose God allowed you to enter into heaven without being holy. What would you do there? Why would you even want to be there? What possible enjoyment would heaven hold for you? Oh, sure, it beats hell. But after your initial fascination wears thin, wouldn't you be terribly bored? Remember, we're talking about spending eternity in this place.

Chris and Phil, two striving young business executives were talking about heaven one day, when Chris surprised Phil by saying, "I don't think you'd want to go."

"What?" Phil exploded. "Are you crazy? Of course I want to go to heaven! Why wouldn't I?"

"Naw; it's not your kind of place."

"Go-wan! Why not?"

"Well," Chris began slowly, "for one thing, I'm not sure that there are any televisions in heaven. What would you do without 'Monday Night Football'?"

"Hey! I'd manage," Phil said with a laugh.

"And I don't think there are going to be any dirty movies or magazines in heaven."

"I could give 'em up," he responded quickly.

"I don't know," Chris answered slowly as he stroked his chin. "Who would you hang out with? What would you do? The people in heaven want to praise and worship God. You're not into that sort of thing, are you?"

"Well, no."

"Would you really be comfortable around a guy like Paul? Or the Apostle John? After you spent most of your life doing the exact things that they spoke and wrote against?"

"Well, maybe not."

"How about Jesus? Would you really want to meet Jesus face-to-face—the One who was crucified because of those same sins that you are still committing today?"

"Well, no," Phil admitted, "but God is love. Doesn't the Bible say that somewhere?"

"Yes, it does," answered Chris. "But are you sure you want to meet Almighty God after you've spent most of your time, money, and energy entertaining His enemies and ignoring His friends?"

"What do you mean?" Phil protested.

"Well, don't you enjoy hanging around with the pleasure-seeking crowd, the materialistic, self-centered, ruthless, profane people in town?"

"Hey, my friends aren't that bad!" Phil retorted.

"Perhaps not," Chris answered, "but don't you realize that there won't be any ungodly people in heaven?"

Phil twisted his mouth into a quizzical expression and asked, "None?"

"None," Chris echoed emphatically.

"I always did say you Christians are a bunch of

fuddie-duddies anyhow. Nobody wants to have any *real fun.*"

"Hmm," Chris pondered. "That might be another problem. You're not fond of fellowshiping with Christians now. But those are the only kinds of people who are going to be in heaven. You don't like to read the Bible; you avoid good preaching like the plague; you can hardly find time during the week for God. When you do go to church, it always seems to be such a chore for you, and when the congregation begins to worship the Lord, you always say, 'Come on! Come on! Let's get on with something more important.' What would somebody like you do in a place where night and day the crowds are singing, 'Holy, Holy, Holy Is the Lord God Almighty'? Come on, Phil. Quit kidding yourself."

Chris paused long enough for his words to sink into Phil's heart. "What in heaven would you do?"

How about you? What in heaven will *you* do, if you are not holy? The answer, of course, is *nothing!* Because without holiness, no man shall see the Lord. Unless you are holy, you will not be there! Perhaps the more accurate and thought-provoking question would be: "What in *hell* will you do if you are not holy?

Again, allow me to ask the difficult question: *Are you holy, or are you unholy?* Better still, ask yourself, *Am I holy, or am I not?*

I am not asking you whether or not you attend church, or have been baptized, or if you have recently taken communion. The question is not even whether you call yourself a Christian. I am asking you the question now that God will ask you on Judgment Day: "Are you holy or are you not?" Of course, He already knows the answer. You probably do, too.

The question is not, "Do you think holiness is a good

idea?" Nor am I asking if you have ever heard a sermon on holiness, or read a book about the subject. I am asking you pointblank: *Are you holy?*

Usually when I ask this question so straightforwardly in public, I can almost predict the responses. One person will say, "Well, yes. I know what the Bible says—that I should be holy—and I'm really thinking about it. Just last week in church, I was under conviction about my lack of holiness. Yessir, I'm giving this matter some serious thought."

When I hear that lame excuse, I often wonder how many poor, lost souls in hell had said something similar.

Holiness does not depend upon what you *think* or what you *feel*. What matters is what you *do* and what you *are*.

Others will say, "Well, you know, we're not all meant to be holy. That's okay for you, but not for me."

Oh? Really? The Bible says, "Every person who has this hope . . . purifies himself . . ." (1 John 3:3).

In my travels, I encounter more than my fair share of theological debaters. Their line is, "I don't believe it is possible for a person to be holy during this lifetime."

My usual reply is, "Then why did God command us to be holy?"

Other well-meaning Christians say, "Ya know, if I were that holy, I would not fit in with a lot of other folks in the world, or even in the church. I might feel out of place."

Probably so.

Still others who have bought the hype about our pluralistic society are concerned about the exclusiveness of holiness. They protest, "If you look at holiness that way, the number of people who are going to be in heaven is not nearly as great as I was led to believe!"

I'd say, "Right again."

I'd say that because that is precisely what Jesus said.

Unfortunately, few people are quoting Him on that point nowadays. Jesus clearly stated, ". . . the gate is wide, and the way is broad that leads to destruction, and many are those who enter by it. For the gate is small, and the way is narrow that leads to life, and few are those who find it" (Matthew 7:13, 14).

Often someone will lament, "You're making Christianity too hard for me!"

On the contrary, if you are rightly discerning the Gospel message, you understand that the biblical, Christian life is actually *impossible* to live under your own power. But for the grace of God, none of us would stand a chance in heaven. Nevertheless, if you neglect or ignore the matter of personal holiness, you will be flirting with what Dietrich Bonhoeffer referred to in *The Cost of Discipleship* as "cheap grace." Bonhoeffer said that many Christians want Christ without the cross. But Jesus said that there is a cross to be taken up daily—not His cross, but yours.

Was Christ crucified *because* of your sin, so you could call yourself by His Name, and yet continue to live in sin? Was He crucified by this world so you could compromise with it?

Never.

Clearly, we are to be saints on earth if we ever hope to be saints in heaven.

From Here to Eternity

His face was flushed and his eyes were flashing as the popular preacher forced his way through a crowd of people, until he stood in front of me. I recognized him immediately—we were guest speakers on the same docket at a midwestern conference—but he was unwilling to wait for formal introductions.

"Young man," he began curtly, "do you mean to tell me that you are teaching these people that they can be holy in this life?"

I was reluctant to respond. He was a renowned and noble spokesman for Christ, highly educated, articulate, and far more qualified to speak upon profound theological issues than I was. His doctrinal positions were much different than my own, but I had studied under his tutelage and profited greatly. Nevertheless, I decided that

I could not back away from what I believed to be true.

"Yes, sir, I am." His eyebrows creased menacingly as I spoke. "But you would not want me to teach them anything less, would you?"

He opened his mouth to respond, then, as though biting a chunk of air, he closed his lips abruptly and walked away.

The next morning I sat in on one of his sessions and heard him publically pray, "Oh Lord, let us live holy lives, just as You have told us You want us to live. And let us live in a manner that Your Word tells us that Christ died to enable us to live, by the power of Your Holy Spirit."

I thought, In thirty seconds or less, he has summed up the thrust of the biblical message of holiness: You cannot live a holy life under your own power; but by the enabling power of the Spirit of Jesus, you can be holy, here and now. This is the consistent message of the Bible. Paul perceived that this holy purpose of God preceded human history. He began his letter to the Ephesians, "Blessed be the God and Father of our Lord Jesus Christ, who has blessed us with every spiritual blessing in the heavenly places in Christ, just as He chose us in Him before the foundation of the world, that we should be holy and blameless before Him" (Ephesians 1:3, 4). From the beginning of time, God's desire seems to have been to develop a people similar in some measure to Himself, with whom He can have eternal and unbroken fellowship.

This can be seen again at the turning point of human history, the cross of Jesus Christ. The writer to the Hebrews explains the ultimate purposes for the crucifixion by stating, "Therefore Jesus also, that He might sanctify the people through His own blood, suffered outside the gate. Hence, let us go out to Him outside the camp, bearing His reproach. For here we do not have a lasting city, but we are seeking the city which is to come" (Hebrews 13:12–14). Not only was Jesus purchasing our salvation when He hung on the cross, but He died that He might sanctify us, that we might be holy, as well.

Those who are sanctified are looking forward to a city. Which city? The same city that we discovered, in the previous chapter, to be holy; a city at the end of history (as we now know it) in which nothing unclean, nothing impure, nothing shameful or abominable shall enter, "but only those whose names are written in the Lamb's Book of Life" (Revelation 21:27). Right down to the last page of the Bible, the message remains the same: "The Spirit and the bride say, 'Come.' And let the one who hears say, 'Come.' And let the one who is thirsty come" (Revelation 22:17). Come where? Come to that ultimate city, the city of God, where nothing impure exists and all is holiness unto the Lord.

Clearly, from before time began (as we know it) to beyond the end of time (as we know it), holiness has been on the heart of your heavenly Father. It is His supreme desire for you.

Practical Holiness

Undoubtedly, the fact that you have read this far indicates that you have a hunger to know more of His holiness in your life. But what does it really mean? What are the nitty-gritty details of the life-style of a holy person supposed to be?

These questions may not be as difficult to answer as you might suppose. If you go back to the original, Mosaic covenant between God and His people (see Exodus 20), you will discover that God established ten easily understood commandments that His holy people are to follow. If you want to live a holy life, you should pay close attention to the moral content of those commands. They are expressions of the will of God, as well as expressions of God's holy nature.

Many Christians would be quick to protest at this point, "Yes, but that is the Old Testament Law."

Okay. Let's think again about the closing pages of the New Testament. Have you ever noticed the people who will not be permitted in that holy city? The cowardly. The unbelieving. The abominable, or the vile people. Murderers. Sexually immoral individuals. Sorcerers, or those who practice black magic or other occult (New Age) arts. All liars (apparently God makes no distinction between little white lies and big, bad, black ones). Those who engage in such activities will have an eternal home, but it is not the kind of place you'd like to visit. John says, "their part will be in the lake that burns with fire and brimstone, which is the second death" (Revelation 21:8). They will be eternally separated from God because they are unholy.

Did you notice the basic content of that list? Those who are excluded from God's Kingdom are those who have violated laws that are surprisingly reminiscent of the original rules of conduct for God's holy people as set down in the Ten Commandments. In case you missed the point, John gives it to you again! In one of the final scenes in Scripture, he says, "Outside are the dogs [which was a common euphemism in John's day for homosexuals] and the sorcerers [which some scholars believe included those who use addictive drugs, since the word sorcerers is translated from the Greek word, pharmakeia, from which pharmacy is derived] and the immoral persons and the murderers and the idolaters, and everyone who loves and practices lying" (Revelation 22:15).

Some skeptics may say, "Yes, but Jesus superceded all of those rules and regulations. He did away with those laws."

Oh? Really?

"Yes," they say, with an ethereal look in their eyes. "Haven't you ever read the Sermon on the Mount or the Beatitudes? Ahhh, the Beatitudes . . . now that's what Christianity is all about!"

When you examine the Beatitudes carefully, however, you discover Jesus describing the people who will be a part of His eternal Kingdom. And who are they? They are:

- "the *poor in spirit*" (Matthew 5:3). They are humble individuals, in whom selfish, sinful pride no longer exists.
- "those who *mourn*" (5:4). Over what do they mourn? Are these mourners merely spiritual crybabies? No. They mourn over the devastating effects of sin, in the world, and in their own lives.
- The meek, "the *gentle*" (5:5). Self-interest no longer reigns in their lives. They have submitted their wills to the will of God and they are now a picture of power under control; their wills are under the control of the Holy Spirit.
- "those who hunger and thirst for righteousness" (5:6). These people love the things God loves and hate the things that God hates.
- "the *merciful*" (5:7). They give themselves away in the Name of Jesus. They forgive much because they know that they have been forgiven much.
- "the *pure in heart*" (5:8). Their desires and motives are unspoiled and holy; they shall see God.

- "the *peacemakers*" (5:9). Which implies that these people have themselves found true peace with God and have become positive instruments of peace in the world.
- the "*persecuted*" (5:10). Those who receive the abuse of sinful society and can still rejoice in their hearts and love with a holy, unconditional love.

These are the kinds of people, Jesus says, who will be in His Kingdom. Then, He proceeds to say something extremely significant. Sadly, it is a statement that most Christians prefer to gloss over, nowadays. Jesus said, "Do not think that I came to abolish the Law or the Prophets; I did not come to abolish, but to fulfill. . . . Whoever then annuls one of the least of these commandments, and so teaches others, shall be called least in the kingdom of heaven; but whoever keeps and teaches them, he shall be called great in the kingdom of heaven (Matthew 5:17, 19). Jesus proceeds, not to do away with the commandments, but to *expand* them!

For example, He says, "You have heard that it was said, 'You shall not commit adultery'; but I say to you, that everyone who looks on a woman to lust for her has committed adultery with her already in his heart" (Matthew 5:27, 28). If you read the remainder of the Sermon on the Mount, you will find in every instance involving attitude and conduct, Jesus did not lower the standards; He raised them.

God is extremely clear about His will for you and how you are supposed to live as a holy person. He spells it out so specifically, you have to wonder how any person could be confused about His requirements. If, somehow, you missed this in the life and ministry of Jesus, God gives you plain and pointed instructions through the pen of the Apostle Paul. Take Paul's letter to the Ephesians for instance: In chapters four and five, Paul writes specific, practical principles as to how holy people are to live.

He says you are to lay aside falsehood (Ephesians 4:25), including those convenient half-truths and selective truths to which you may be prone. Speak the truth, rather than lying.

When you get angry, don't let the sun go down without getting it resolved and don't give the devil an opportunity to gain a foothold in your life or anyone else's life, as a result of anger (Ephesians 4:26, 27).

To the person who is stealing, Paul speaks quite candidly: "Quit it!" You must not steal (Ephesians 4:28). Whether it is bringing home pencils from work, or pocketing extra sugars and napkins at your favorite fast food restaurant, it's stealing, and you are not to do it. Whether you steal from another person's paper at school or work, steal from the government by cheating on your income tax, or steal from God by not paying your tithes and offerings, you are a thief.

Many churches steal sheet music by photocopying copyrighted material for use by their church choirs. It's okay, they assume, because they are using the stolen material for God's glory. Ha! Try that logic at your local bank. Other Christians, who would shrink at the thought of burglarizing the local video store or record outlet have no qualms at all about illegally duplicating copyrighted video cassettes, records, and tapes.

Paul says, "Don't steal; in fact, if you are able, get out there and *work!*" Do something useful with your life. Instead of pirating someone else's work, or sponging off another person, stop being a parasite and start working so you will have something to share with those who are in need (Ephesians 4:28).

The Apostle also talks about your conversation (Ephe-

sians 4:29). He says, keep it positive. Why? So others may
be edified and built up.

Test yourself today. After each of your conversations,
ask yourself, "Will that person with whom I have been
talking go away a better person or a worse person because
of our discussion?" Will he or she be built up, encouraged, and edified? Or will that person feel as though he or
she had been dragged through the mire and the mud? The
words of a positively holy person should have an uplift-
ing impact upon other people. Even when you must
speak about negative matters, if at all possible, put that
conversation into a positive context, and *always* end your
discussion on a positive note.

Paul provides the overriding principle that should
govern your life-style when he says, "And do not grieve
the Holy Spirit of God" (Ephesians 4:30). This key is
crucial to holy living. When a person is filled with the
Holy Spirit and is living with his or her life under the
control of the Spirit who is Holy, a holy life-style is the
inevitable result.

Paul describes more specifics of that sort of life-style.
He says, "Let all bitterness and wrath and anger and
clamor and slander be put away from you, along with all
malice. And be kind to one another, tender-hearted,
forgiving each other, just as God in Christ also has
forgiven you" (Ephesians 4:31, 32).

Moreover, Paul tells us to "be imitators of God" (Ephesians 5:1). Fine. But what is God like? God is holy. As one
of His children, then, you should be holy. That means
you are to "walk in love" (5:2). John Wesley understood
this. Perhaps that is why he referred to holiness as
"perfect love." Holy men and women are to love as Christ
loved, and Christ loved so unselfishly that He "gave

Himself up for us [as] an offering and a sacrifice to God"
(5:2). That is how you are to love.

Consequently, there should not even be a hint of
immorality, impurity, or greed in a holy person's life
(Ephesians 5:3). As a representative of Christ, there
should be no filthiness, silly talk, or coarse jesting, but
rather the positive expression of thanks (5:4). Paul pulls
no punches; he says straightforwardly, "For this you
know with certainty, that no immoral or impure person or
covetous man, who is an idolator, has an inheritance in
the kingdom of Christ and God" (5:5).

Divine Déjà Vu

Okay—it's quiz time. Did you happen to notice how
many of the Ten Commandments are included in Paul's
discussion of positive holiness? If you study the passage
carefully, you will find that all ten of the commandments
found in Exodus are repeated directly or implied in
Paul's letter to the Ephesians. The only command that is
excluded is "Remember the Sabbath." Even that one may
be implied by the principle "Grieve not the Spirit," for if
you have an improper regard for the Sabbath, you undoubtedly will grieve the Holy Spirit. Similarly, if you
disobey your parents by lying, cheating, losing your
temper, stealing, cursing or otherwise speaking unwhole-
some words, being unforgiving, immoral, or impure, you
have obviously violated the fifth commandment, which is
to honor your parents.

God's Word is marvelously consistent. He has no
hidden agenda when it comes to how His holy people are
to live. In fact, the Lord is so clear and specific it hurts. He
desires a holy people. That has been His plan since before
the foundation of the earth; that was His purpose in

providing the cross of Christ, and that will be His plan for all who will enter His heavenly, holy city, the New Jerusalem.

Of course, that is precisely why you need Jesus so desperately. Because without Him, you stand no chance of ever being holy. You don't get holy by legalistically keeping God's commandments. You obey His commandments *because* you are holy. It follows, then, that the Holy Spirit is the only One who can make you holy and give you the power to honestly live the way God has commanded.

Therefore, if you are to have fellowship with a holy God, you must allow Him to cleanse your heart by faith and to fill you with His holy presence. When you do, it will be the turning point in your Christian life. It was that and much more for a young Presbyterian missionary named John Hyde.

John had grown up as a "preacher's kid." He had dutifully gone to a Christian college, then on to seminary, and had volunteered for missionary service in India. When he boarded the ship in New York City, enroute to his new home, he paused to check through his mail and found a letter from a friend of his father. He thought, *Great! He is wishing me well.* But as he opened the envelope and began to read, John discovered that the paper contained a much more poignant message.

It was a moving letter, as the man wrote to John of his loving concern for him. The friend told the young man how he had prayed for him for many years, and how he would continue to do so now that John had answered the call to foreign missionary service.

Then came the clincher. He included in his letter this word of warning: "John, do not go to India unless you know what it means to be filled with the Holy Spirit.

Because you will need the fullness of God and a clean heart, if you are to be effective there."

John Hyde read those words and became indignant. *Who does he think he is?* thought John. *I'm the one who is going to the mission field. I'm the one who is sticking my life on the line. I'm the one who is obeying Christ. He's the guy who is staying at home! What right does he have to talk to me like this?*

He took the letter, crumpled it up, and threw it down on the deck of the ship. Then he stormed on his way to his stateroom aboard the steamer. But the Holy Spirit began speaking to John, chastening him and rebuking him. Finally, Hyde went back up on deck and found the note right where he had thrown it. He picked up the letter and took it back to his cabin. He unwrinkled the paper as best he could, spread it out on his bed, and got down on his knees beside the bunk.

He prayed, "God, if I am not filled with the Holy Spirit, I want You to fill me now."

He felt a little better, but nothing of significance happened. Although he gave himself to prolonged periods of prayer for the remainder of the voyage, John arrived in India still uncertain of his own spiritual status and lacking spiritual power.

Nevertheless, he was determined to do the work of God. Dutifully, he devoted himself to intensive Bible study, language study, visitation, and prayer. He did all the things that a good missionary should do, yet there was still an emptiness in his soul, and his best efforts were mostly ineffective.

One day, John heard another missionary preaching about the power of Jesus' blood to cleanse a person from all sin. When the man finished speaking, a Hindu confronted him and said, "Sir, you spoke about the power of

Jesus' blood to cleanse a man from all sin. Tell me. Has He cleansed you from all sin?"

John Hyde had been standing close by and when he heard the Hindu man's question, it seemed as though his own heart leaped into his throat. He said later, "I was scared to death that he was going to turn and look at me and ask that same question. Because there was one area of defeat that I had never conquered—no—that I had never let Christ give me victory in."

John Hyde knew that he needed to get alone with God, so he beat a hasty retreat to his room. There, he got down on his knees and prayed, "Lord, if You can't do something for me more than what You have done, I'm going to book passage back to the United States. I will not stay here, unless You give me victory over sin within my heart."

Apparently, God did, because John Hyde stayed. Not only did he stay, but he became one of the most influential lives to ever touch India. His contributions to that country were arguably of far greater value from an eternal perspective than those of Ghandi, for John Hyde was a famous "prayer warrior" and a faithful and effective witness for Jesus Christ. He prayed so much and so fervently that people began calling him "Praying Hyde." More impressive, perhaps, were God's answers to "Praying Hyde's" specific prayers.

For example, in 1908, John prayed that at least one person each day would come into a relationship with Christ through the work of his mission. That year, four hundred people entrusted their lives to the Lord. The next year, John prayed for two people each day to be saved, and they were! The following year, his faith flourishing, Hyde prayed for four people each day to be brought into Christ's Kingdom through his mission's efforts. God answered the prayers of John Hyde, because his heart was cleansed and his life was holy.

Perhaps you need a cleansing similar to that. Maybe you need to be empowered, that your prayers would be answered and that your service for the Savior would be effective.

Are you aware of spiritual failure in your life? Is there conscious disobedience to the Ten Commandments or Jesus' expansion of them? The issue is not how badly you have sinned or how blatantly you have broken His moral law. The question is: Have you *ever* sinned? If you have ever disobeyed His Word, you desperately need a Savior.

Are you living in holiness? If your answer is not a certain, joyful, whole-hearted, "Yes!", why not? You know His standards, and you have seen in this chapter that His laws have not changed and will not change. He asks only for your permission to allow Him to change *you*. He is able to do that. He is willing to cleanse you, to fill you with His holiness, to keep you from falling, and to give you the power to live positively and purely from here to eternity.

11

Charting Your Course

The medical missionary's small boat crashed through another massive wave, drenching the man and everything in the tiny vessel that was not covered by canvas or stored in one of the craft's compartments. The night was dark and stormy—the kind of night that sailors describe when they are telling scary stories, only this was the real thing.

The sea raged against the rugged man's efforts to keep the boat from capsizing. The rain, wrapped in a cold, whistling wind, pelted his face as he attempted to guide the little vessel up the Canadian North Atlantic coast. Inky darkness and thick fog conspired to suck up the beam of the boat's small light, leaving the missionary in almost total blackness. He could not see where he was going, so he had no other choice but to navigate according to his compass.

If it had not been for his dedication to the Lord, the medical missionary would have quickly turned his boat around and headed for home. But he had received an urgent call that said he was desperately needed. One of the villagers was dying and the missionary was his only chance.

As he battled through the murky waters, the missionary began to be concerned that something was seriously wrong. *I should have reached my destination by now,* he worried. Yet as he peered into the darkness, there was no land to be seen, and his sailor's "sixth sense" detected nothing solid nearby. Suddenly, to his horror and surprise, he realized the answer to his problem. He was not moving northward, toward his goal, as his compass had indicated; he was headed due east, straight out into the open sea! Desperately, he wrestled against the furious wind and waves and finally was able to turn the small craft back toward less frenzied waters and eventually to shore.

The next day, the missionary carefully examined his boat for damages and discovered, to his chagrin, the reason for his compass's inaccurate readings. He had recently taken the boat into dry dock for repairs, part of which required that the compass be replaced. Apparently, when the man who was installing the new directional equipment was setting the screws that held the compass in place, he ran out of pure brass screws. Assuming that a slight compromise would be insignificant, he found a screw made of a ferrous alloy and finished the job with that.

Consequently, the magnetic tip of the compass was attracted to the alloyed metal and could not produce consistently true readings. The missionary discovered, almost tragically too late, that while he thought he had been charting his course by the magnetic North Pole, the craft had actually been charting its own course. It was an accident just waiting to happen.

A self-orientation exists within the unsanctified human heart that is quite similar to the boat with a defective compass. Unless you have allowed Christ to correct the problem, there is an egocentric nature about you that tends to chart your own course. Beware: Your inner compass is giving you inaccurate, undependable readings. If you stubbornly insist upon following its faulty information, you will inevitably choose a deflected course that will lead you to despair, disorientation, discouragement—and ultimately to destruction.

John Dawson, director of Youth With a Mission's Southwestern United States operations, is a friend and fellow Bible teacher from whom I have benefited greatly. John has a favorite saying: "Heart is smart," by which he means, trust your heart and you won't go too far wrong. In fact, most of the time you will be right on target. I have tested John's theory, and it works . . . usually.

Perhaps, though, an adjective ought to be included along with John's acute insight. Maybe we should say, "A holy heart is smart" or "A clean, Christ-centered heart is smart." Unless your heart is cleansed by the blood of Christ, you run a severe risk of basing your heart-felt intuitions and conclusions upon deceptive affections. Even with the best intentions, unless your heart is holy, it is possible to believe that you are seeking that which is pure and true, when, in fact, you have been deceived and have been chasing after that which is tainted with the impurity of self-concern and self-importance. Tragically, the cause of Christ has suffered horrible setbacks because of this self-centeredness, and some Christians have completely capsized as a result.

The Great Paradox

No doubt that is one reason why Paul describes the way of holiness as a paradox: It is life out of death. He says in Galatians 2:20, "I have been crucified with Christ; and it is no longer I who live, but Christ lives in me; and the life which I now live in the flesh I live by faith in the Son of God, who loved me, and delivered Himself up for me."

Obviously, Paul is not talking about being physically dead and buried. He is referring to a death of your self-orientation, a crushing of that incorrect, egocentric compass by which you have been charting your course. Positively, he means the emplacement of Christ as the Navigator upon whom you depend for guidance.

"Is this really possible?" you may be asking. "Can I really 'reckon myself as *dead*;' or am I merely playing with spiritual semantics?" R. A. Torrey, the great evangelist from the past, had similar questions. Although Torrey thoroughly believed and preached the possibility of being "baptized with the Holy Spirit" and encouraged an emphasis upon spiritual gifts in the life of every Spirit-filled Christian, he did not believe that a person's carnal nature could be put to death. Nor do many modern churchmen believe that a person can be delivered from the bondage of sin. Their credo is: "I sin every day in thought, word, or deed."

Some scholars, however, see things differently. In his book, *The Holy Spirit in the Latter Days*, Dr. Harold Lindsell, former editor of *Christianity Today* and a thorough-going Protestant Reformation thinker, sounds closer to John Wesley at some points than he does to Mr. Torrey. Lindsell summarizes the extreme elements of the centuries-old debate between the two largest theological camps, the Arminians and the Calvinists:

The Arminian. . . . is saying that when the believer is filled with the Holy Spirit he *cannot* sin; the Calvinist, on the other hand, seems to be saying that whether the believer is or is not filled with the Holy Spirit, he *will* sin in word, thought, and deed every day. There is a third option, however, which differs from both of these in a material sense, and it may provide a better answer to this difference of opinion. It can be stated this way: the believer may sin but *he does not have to.*[1]

Still, many contemporary, "Reformed" theologians seriously question any "crisis experience" subsequent to salvation. They are quite willing to talk about "growing more Christ-like," but they are extremely reluctant to declare themselves as dead to self or dead to sin.

Why does such confusion and diversity of opinion exist about something so obviously biblical? Is it really possible to be crucified with Christ? I queried Dr. Dennis Kinlaw along these same lines.

As president of Asbury College and former president of the Christian Holiness Association, Dr. Kinlaw is eminently qualified to speak on these subjects. He has made a lifelong study of biblical holiness and is highly esteemed as a brilliant but practical interpreter of the Bible. A kind man, unassuming, and always tolerant of those whose theological positions and presuppositions are different from his own, Dr. Kinlaw uses an intriguing phrase to explain how it is possible that the self can be crucified. He repeatedly refers to "the tyranny of the self-interest."

In Dr. Kinlaw's estimation, that self-interest is really at the heart of sin. For example, even in the Garden of Eden, before Adam and Eve willfully rebelled against God's Word, before they disobeyed His revealed will, they succumbed to self-interest. Both of their attitudes were "I want what *I* want." This tyranny of the self-interest, says Dr. Kinlaw, *can* be cleansed by the blood of Christ through His Holy Spirit. The implication is if self-interest is the precursor to sin and its power can be beaten then the predilection to sin itself can be prevented. Of course, it is still *possible* to sin, but one whose self-interest has been cleansed is not nearly so prone to do so; he or she is no longer obligated to sin.

Is All Self-Interest Sinful?

Please understand that interest in one's self does not necessarily have to be sinful. A certain amount of self-esteem is right and proper for every person. It is when *self*-interest runs counter to God's interests and God's will for your life that it leads to sin.

In a sense, as long as you are breathing, you can never be totally devoid of self-interest, nor should you desire to be. You will always be interested in taking care of yourself, and as a person of value and a person for whom Christ died, you owe that to yourself and to Him! Perhaps that is why the best self-improvement programs speak to something deep within you that says, "Yes! I want to change. I want to be a better person than I am presently."

Frankly, you *can* change many of the negative concepts you have about yourself. At this point, much to the dismay of some naive, anti-intellectual, or narrow-minded individuals, modern pop psychology has something important to say: You can improve your self-image. Many devout believers need to do so. You can change some of the externals about your demeanor, such as the way you dress, the manner in which you comb your hair, the care you take of your body, the way you speak (to others and to yourself), and the way you carry yourself. By attending to these areas, you will have a positive impact upon the way you feel about yourself. But watch out! Here is where the subtle error can creep in on you.

Although you *may* improve your self-image through pop psychology, *you will never be able to deliver yourself from self-centeredness*, or as Dr. Kinlaw says, from "the tyranny of the self-interest." You grievously err if you think that you can set yourself free through your own power, intelligence, or self-effort. This is the fundamental misconception of secular humanism: that human beings are basically good, and given enough time, even sinful men and women will become altruistic; they will work things out sufficiently and will sacrifice their own self-interest on the altar of what is good for mankind. A noble thought. Unfortunately, thousands of years of historical evidence prove otherwise. Such utopian jibberish usually leads to the exclusion of God and the dethronement of Jesus Christ, to selfish manipulation of others, to pride, and to sin.

The best way to deal with your legitimate self-concern is to put it under the control of absolute love, Christ's love. Then, the tyranny of self-interest *will* be broken. That is precisely what Paul was talking about when he said that he was "crucified with Christ" (Galatians 2:20). Pop psychology or works-oriented self-improvement programs will never be able to do that for you. It must take a crucifixion. Furthermore, you cannot "crucify" yourself. One hand will always be free. You must allow God to do this; you must be crucified *with* Christ.

Does this sound a little frightening? Let me assure you that it is! But it is also the way of fullness and fruitfulness in the Kingdom of God.

One of the modern-day saints who found this to be true

(and as a result, will most assuredly be included along with the spiritual giants of the faith by future generations) was the late E. Stanley Jones.

Jones became a Christian as a young man, and for the first year of his new-found life, he lived under what he called "cloudless skies." Then he began to notice something that bothered him. He said, "After a year of unalloyed joy I found something alien began to rise from the cellar of my life. I felt there was something down there not in alignment with this new life I had found—ugly tempers, moodiness, deep-down conflicts. The general tenor of life was victory, but there were disturbing intrusions from the depths. I was becoming a house divided against itself. I was puzzled, confused, hurt with a tinge of disappointment."[2]

E. Stanley Jones pondered the questions that perhaps have haunted you: "Was this the best that Christianity could do—to leave me wrestling with myself, or with something alien to myself? What was this dark something within?"

Jones coined an interesting term for this "dark something within." Theologians had referred to it as the "old man," or "the flesh," or the "carnal mind." He called it the "unconverted subconscious." He agreed with the psychologists of his day who identified three basic drives in a person: self, sex, and the herd, and he saw his own need for deliverance in those three areas.

The self, according to Jones, is that desire deep within a person that demands to be dominant. It causes one to assert himself or herself, imperiously surging forth in a self-seeking search for personal satisfaction, indifferent to the needs and desires of others. Sex, of course, plays a leading role in almost every aspect of modern society. The herd, or the social instinct, is the desire for acceptance from those around you, causing you to do many things merely because "everybody else is doing it." These drives within you naturally tend to usurp the place of God's Spirit in your life.

Jones concluded that all three drives, regardless of their particular manifestations, are centered in the self. He described immoral sexual urges as "the self's desire for pleasure," and the tendency to comply with the herd as "self's desire for protection, through conformity." Basically, he said, " 'innate depravity' is the self surrendered to nothing except itself—the self become God."[3]

That is how E. Stanley Jones saw the crisis within himself; he was, in his own words, "stymied by this inner conflict." Then one day, he picked up and began to read Hannah Whitall Smith's classic book, *The Christian's Secret of a Happy Life*, and his "heart was kindled with desire." Through reading this book, Jones began to discover how he could find deliverance from—and victory over—himself. He said:

> I wasn't reading it; I was eating it. I got to the forty-second page when God spoke to me: "Now is the time to find." I pleaded: "Lord, I don't know what I want. This book is telling me. Let me read the book first and then I can intelligently seek." But the voice was imperious: "Now is the time to find." I tried to read on, but the words were blurred. I saw I was in a controversy with God, so I closed the book, dropped on my knees beside my bed, and said: "Now, Lord, what shall I do?" And He replied: "Will you give me your all?" And after a moment's hesitation I replied: "Yes, Lord, of course I will. I will give you my all, all I know and all I don't know." Then he replied: "Then take my all, take the Holy Spirit." I paused for a moment: my all for his all; my all was myself, his all was himself,

the Holy Spirit. I saw in a flash the offer. I eagerly replied: "I will take the Holy Spirit." I arose from my knees, with no evidence, save his word. . . . I walked around the room repeating my acceptance. The doubts began to close in on me. I did what Abraham did when the birds came to scatter his sacrifice—he shooed them away. I walked around the room pushing away with my hands the menacing doubts. When suddenly I was filled with the Holy Spirit. Wave after wave of the Spirit seemed to be going through me as a cleansing fire. I could only walk the floor with the tears of joy flowing down my cheeks. I could do nothing but praise him—and did. I knew this was no passing emotion; the Holy Spirit had come to abide with me forever.

He had been with me, with me in the conscious mind in conversion. Now he was in me, in me in the subconscious. . . . Now the subconscious was redeemed. These drives which reside in the subconscious—self, sex, and the herd—were cleansed. . . .[4]

E. Stanley Jones emphasized that these basic inclinations were not eliminated; nor were they merely suppressed or rendered inoperative. They were *cleansed* and *consecrated* to the purposes of God. He explained, "The self, dedicated to Christ, now expresses itself as the servant of all, thus becoming the greatest of all; sex, now dedicated to the creative God, becomes creative. . . . The herd urge, now emancipated by surrender to God from subservience to society, can serve and love society. . . . Delivered from the people, you can now serve them—and only then!"[5]

E. Stanley Jones experienced what the Apostle Paul described as being "crucified with Christ." The tyranny of the self-interest in him had been broken. As a result,

God used him as a mighty messenger in America and as an effective missionary in India.

Cracked Mirrors

Admittedly, crucifixion of the self is a difficult concept to understand. Often, in the history of the Church, it has been downplayed, neglected, or ignored. That's not surprising; one of the most basic tenets of Christianity, justification by faith, suffered such an ignominious fate for years. It took the courage and nonconformity and Christ-centered convictions of Martin Luther to uncover the truth that men and women are not saved by works or through the rituals of the Church; they are saved by sheer faith in Jesus Christ alone (Romans 1:17). It is only by His good grace that any person can be saved or sanctified (Ephesians 2:8).

This points out a rather provocative and pernicious problem, but one that the person who is seeking to please God will surely encounter sooner or later: You cannot always accurately interpret what is *biblically* correct by looking only at the Church. Nor is it wise to establish your personal standards by the conduct of contemporary Christians. The only safe guide by which you can gauge your spiritual progress is the Scripture itself. The Bible alone is the unerring compass by which the Christian Church and Christian conduct can be compared and your own course can be charted.

You may look at your church or other Christians in your community and say, "They seem quite content to compromise; I guess I can too." Keep in mind, though, that when you stand before the Lord to take your "final examinations," you will not be judged on the basis of your church or community standards. You will be judged according to Jesus Christ and His holiness.

Change of Heart

The recurring theme of the New Testament is that it is a relatively easy thing to *become* a Christian; it is much more difficult to *be* Christian in thought, word, attitudes, and life-style. Similarly, there are many believers about whom the noun *Christian* may be applicable, but the adjective *Christian* is highly inaccurate.

This was the Apostle Paul's concern for his converts. He not only wanted them to call themselves Christians; he wanted them to live in a Christ-like manner. To the Romans, he wrote, "Therefore do not let sin reign in your mortal body that you should obey its lusts, and do not go on presenting the members of your body to sin as instruments of unrighteousness; but present yourselves to God as those alive from the dead. . . . For sin shall not be master over you . . ." (Romans 6:12–14).

Paul presents here the emancipation proclamation for every saint. He says that it is possible, by the grace of God, to live in such a way that sin will not have dominion over you. He doggedly presses his point with impeccable and hard-hitting logic. He asks, "Do you not know that when you present yourselves to someone as slaves for obedience, you are slaves of the one whom you obey, either of sin resulting in death, or of obedience resulting in righteousness?" (Romans 6:16).

Then Paul says something that is absolutely astounding: "But thanks be to God that though you were slaves of sin, you became obedient from the heart. . . . and having been freed from sin, you became slaves of righteousness. . . . But now having been freed from sin and enslaved to God, you derive your benefit, resulting in sanctification, and the outcome, eternal life" (Romans 6:17, 18, 22). The amazing aspect of this statement is Paul's use of the past tense to describe the believer's relationship to sin. You *were* slaves to sin, but now, *having been freed,* you have become slaves to God. Notice, too, the results of this freedom: sanctification (holiness) and eternal life.

It is no accident that the climax of the passage concludes: "For the wages of sin is death, but the free gift of God is eternal life in Christ Jesus our Lord" (Romans 6:23). Clearly, sin is incompatible with our holy God; He hates it, whether it is in the life of an unbeliever or in the heart of a person who bears His Name. That is why Paul insists that you must not continue to live in sin; its consequences are deadly; it will damn you.

Moreover, God desires that you be holy, that you be delivered from the dominance of self-interest, sin, and death. As you surrender to His control, He wants to place you under the direction of His Holy Spirit. He wants to fill you up to where you no longer live on the dregs of your own spiritual resources. Instead, you can depend upon *His* supernatural supply, which will perpetually fill your heart to overflowing.

When you allow Him to do this in you, it will be as radical as the difference between night and day. Paul graphically delineates the distinctions between life "in the Spirit" and life "in the flesh" in his letter to the Galatians. He said:

Now the deeds of the flesh are evident, which are: immorality, impurity, sensuality, idolatry, sorcery, enmities, strife, jealousy, outbursts of anger, disputes, dissensions, factions, envying, drunkenness, carousing, and

*things like these, of which I forewarn you just as I have
forewarned you that those who practice such things shall
not inherit the kingdom of God. But the fruit of the Spirit
is love, joy, peace, patience, kindness, goodness, faithfulness, gentleness, self-control; against such things there is
no law. Now those who belong to Christ Jesus have
crucified the flesh with its passions and desires*

Galatians 5:19–24

Notice Paul is contrasting a life controlled by self-interest against a life controlled by the Spirit of Christ. When you live to satisfy yourself, you will inevitably find that you are an enemy of God. But when you allow the Holy Spirit to possess you completely, the character of holiness—the fruit of the Spirit—will be produced in your life.

How can you experience this? Begin by *yielding* yourself to His Holy Spirit. Stop presenting yourself as a slave to sin and start presenting yourself as a slave to righteousness. Sounds simple, doesn't it?

Unfortunately, it is not. Because precisely at the point where the Spirit of God asks you to surrender, you will begin to understand how sinful you really are. You may see, for the first time in your Christian life, how little you truly trust Christ. Your unbelief and destructive doubt will never loom any larger than the moment when the Spirit of Jesus asks you to hand over the keys of your life to Him.

F. B. Meyer found this to be true. F. B. Meyer was one of the most beloved Baptist preachers who ever lived. Besides a busy preaching schedule, he served as president of the World Baptist Alliance. His ministry had a profound impact during his lifetime, and his books continue to bless, challenge, and encourage Christians today.

He had been in the ministry for several years before he had heard a message on how a man or woman could experience holiness of heart. Immediately he began to seek that blessing for himself. As he sought to be filled with the Holy Spirit, it seemed to F. B. Meyer that God was saying to him, "All right Meyer; give Me the keys to your heart. You told Me that you wanted Me to have your life; let Me have your *whole* life. Give Me the key ring with all the keys to your life."

Meyer said, "Surely, Lord," as he stealthily slipped one key off the ring and then handed God the remaining keys.

The Lord said to him, "Meyer, what is that in your hand?"

"Lord, that's very insignificant," the preacher answered. "It's just a small key to a small lock to a small room that has almost nothing in it."

The Lord said, "I thought you wanted Me to have your *whole* life?"

"That's right, Lord!"

"I can't have your whole life," God said, "unless you give it all to Me."

Meyer remained stubborn. "Can't I have even a corner left?"

The Lord replied patiently, "No. If you want Me to have your whole life, you can't have a corner left."

Meyer continued to hedge, "Lord, that key is to something so inconsequential . . . ."

But the Lord would not budge. He said, "You are not wholly Mine until you give Me that key." Then He said something to F. B. Meyer that He has undoubtedly said to you. God said, "Really, if you are unwilling to give Me *that* key, there is no point in giving Me all the others."

F. B. Meyer said, "I thought I would die. Worse still, I found that I *couldn't* give it to Him; I didn't have the power. Then, for the first time in my life, I found the unbelief and the resistance in me toward God . . . and I was a minister of the Gospel!"

He said, "God, this is frightful. In my impotence, I am unable to give it. Lord, can You take it?"

The Lord graciously answered, "If you will give Me permission. Are you *willing* to be willing to give it to Me?"

F. B. Meyer surrendered himself to God and said, "Lord, if You can, take it!"

Meyer recalled, "I thought I would die, but He took it. Then He opened that door and exposed me to all of the self in its carnal, fleshly, lust and evil; and began to clean me out and began to fill me."

Later, F. B. Meyer looked back and said, "God did not do that to hurt me. God did that to help me. Because that little corner represented my dominance over my life and my hindrance to His plan for me."

Have you given God all the keys to your life? Or do you find within yourself that same fear, unbelief, and resistance that F. B. Meyer did? You know, don't you, that God wants all the keys? He will not allow you to hide one behind your back. He knows the significance of that small key to that small lock to the small room. He knows what is rotting within that room, and His desire is to make a clean sweep of your life; to wipe out the dirt and the cobwebs, to open you up to the light, and to allow the fresh wind of His Spirit to revitalize that area of your life as well as the other rooms that you have already opened to Him.

You need not fear giving your life to Him unreservedly. He does not want to hurt you. He loves you and wants the best for you. Yet, that is the reason He insists upon having absolute control. You may be the quarterback on this team, but He is the Owner and the Coach; and He calls the plays.

Ask yourself some serious questions:

1. Do I trust Jesus?
2. Do I honestly believe that He loves me and wants the best for me?
3. Would Jesus ever do anything, or ask me to do anything, that would not be in my ultimate best interests?
4. Doesn't it make sense to surrender the control of my life to Him?

Undoubtedly, if you experience reluctance in letting go of the controls of your life, it is because of the irreversible nature of the commitment that He is asking you to make. Crucifixion is so . . . so *final!* Perhaps you would prefer to have some reservations about your commitment to Christ, just in case this holy life is not all that it is cracked up to be. Maybe in the secret compartments of your heart and mind, you contemplate some subsequent circumstance or situation that might cause you to want to withdraw from this contract. *Can't I condition His control? you wonder. Listen Lord, You can go this far in my life, but I want the right to pull back at any point.*

That attitude will never lead you to holiness. In fact, that mind-set is what the Bible calls "carnal" or "fleshly"; it is the unwillingness to make a final, complete, irreversible, "yes" commitment to Jesus Christ.

Of course, it is possible to go spiritually A.W.O.L. ("Absent Without Leave") at any point in your Christian life. The spiritual plane does not exist where you cannot disobey, where you cannot sin, where you cannot reverse your commitment. None of the truly great saints ever endorsed a doctrine that said they *could not* sin. Even

John Wesley, the founder of the Methodists, whose teaching of "Perfect Love" has often been maligned and misinterpreted as sinless perfection, plainly stated that there is no spiritual state from which a believer cannot fall.

Certainly, it is possible to renege. But what Christ wants from you is a promise that you *will not* reverse your stand.

Almost Persuaded

At this point, some Christians say, "I'm not sure I can make a commitment such as that. I surely don't want to lie to God and make a vow I will not keep."

Others are more fearful: "I don't want to disappoint the Lord, or let Him down by failing to keep my promises."

Make the promise. He will enable you to keep it. Remember: "Faithful is He who calls you, and *He* also will bring it to pass" (1 Thessalonians 5:24). Always keep in mind that it is His power, and His alone, that allows you the ability to live a holy life. Your holiness is derived from Him and is dependent upon Him.

If you desire to experience true holiness, you must come to the place where you are willing to yield your will completely to Christ. Without that total, radical commitment, you will find yourself repeatedly getting close to entering into His fullness, and then backing off in fear. Many devout Christians spin their wheels in perpetual spiritual frustration and despair because they refuse to cross the line and "sell out" to Jesus. Consequently, they run from church to church, conference to conference, seminar to seminar, continually seeking some new, exciting experience, hoping to find spiritual satisfaction some other, easier way. They won't find it. They may get confused by a counterfeit or sucked in by a deceiver, but they will not discover God's secret to spiritual success . . . not until they are willing to make a complete, categorical, irrevocable, commitment to Christ.

This may be one reason why you are finding yourself spiritually anemic, consecrating and reconsecrating, dedicating and rededicating, yet still coming away dissatisfied. Surely, you should always be sensitive to the Spirit of God, and if He bids you to make a fresh dedication of your life, you should do so at once. Sometimes, though, it is all too easy to step around the real issue—He is bidding you to die to yourself and to make an absolute surrender.

At a pastor's conference in Kentucky, Paul Rees rattled his audience when he revealed:

> Quite candidly, I am one of those who believe that we have done an untold damage to the entire cause of Christian sanctity by the fuzzy and sloppy way we handle this matter of consecration, or as it is often expressed, 'reconsecration'! Too many people go to consecration services, kneel at consecration altars, sing the reconsecration hymns, and then go out just as they were before. Let me make myself clear: I don't mean that they need to go out exactly as they were before; I only meant to say that this whole idea of a consecration is so shallow that it needs to be done over and over and over again. This is contrary to the profound moral intensity and finality of the Book of Romans where the believer makes his total response to the total demand of God for holiness of heart and life.

God wants you to make up your mind. You are going to have to choose who will be lord of your life. Jesus said, "I know your deeds, that you are neither cold nor hot; I would that you were cold or hot. So because you are lukewarm, and neither hot nor cold, I will spit you out of My mouth" (Revelation 3:15, 16).

Now, that's painful. It hurts so badly because it hits right where we live. It forces us out of our wishy-washy, compromising, half-hearted commitments to Christ and demands that we decide to whom we will give our unswerving allegiance.

Some people are honestly troubled about making what Andrew Murray referred to as an "absolute surrender." They insist, "How can I surrender tomorrow when I have no idea what tomorrow will hold? I'll have to wait until tomorrow comes, and then I will see whether or not I can give it to God."

Consider this: God is not overly concerned about your tomorrows. In fact, He is not troubled about your todays. He *knows* what is in your tomorrow, and He sees where you are at today. He is not talking to you about a surrender of your past, present, or future. Nor is He asking you to lay down things, events, circumstances, places, or people; although all of these issues are involved. God is asking you to surrender your *self*, to allow that tyranny of self-interest to be broken by the blood of Christ, and to allow His Spirit to take over the guidance system of your life.

12

Dead Men Have No Rights

A friend of mine should write horror stories for a living. She certainly has enough material. She works in a morgue. Every time we talk about her job, she always has another nightmarish tale to tell.

One day, when I was speaking at a conference near her place of employment, I stopped at the hospital, just to see the setting of her outrageous sagas. The woman on duty at the information desk pointed me in the right direction. "Go down the hall, make a left, and take the last elevator down as far as you can go," she instructed icily. "I'll call 'em to tell 'em that yer on yer way."

"Thank you, ma'am," I attempted to say cheerily and with a smile. Her face remained rigid. "Have a wonderful day," I ventured. Still no response from the receptionist. *If you can,* I thought, turning toward the hallway she had indicated.

I passed through the spotless, sterile corridor of the hospital and began to get nervous. While pressing the "Down" button to the loneliest elevator I had ever seen, I started to seriously doubt the wisdom of my visit. *What if she's busy?* I wondered. *What if they are working on a body?* I really wasn't in the mood for an autopsy.

Reluctantly, I stepped inside the elevator and stood back as the doors clunked shut behind me. *Not much room in here,* I noted as I hastily pressed the button marked "B." *Basement,* I assumed.

Few elevator rides in my life seemed any longer than that one. As the suspended cubbyhole creakily crept toward the cellar, my mind filled with creepy stories my friend had told me. "Sometimes," she said, "strange things hapen. Occasionally, a 'live' nerve ending will cause a body to twitch, even though the person is legally dead." One such occurrence nearly gave her a heart attack, she admitted. Apparently, she had been transporting a dead body from the emergency room to the morgue by means of the elevator. She wheeled the hospital gurney into the cramped elevator, pressed the button, and moved behind the gurney, with her back up against the wall, so she could push the stretcher out the elevator door when it opened. Suddenly, the corpse sat straight up on the stretcher! She fainted. When the dead man's muscles relaxed, he "died" again.

As I was recalling my friend's horrible experience, the elevator in which I was riding jolted to a halt, and I quickly shifted toward the exit. The doors waited an extremely long time before opening—at least it seemed that way to me. Finally, they crawled aside, and I could escape the claustrophobic closet.

A chill was the first thing that struck me, as I stepped out of the elevator and into the morgue. Then I noticed the dim lighting, almost as if it was too cold for the fluorescent bulbs to fully function. One flickering light caused a type of strobe light effect in the eerie room.

"Hello . . ." I called into the gloominess.

No answer.

"Hello . . ." I called again, slightly louder. "Anybody home?" I said, before I realized the foolishness of my question. I stepped further into the room and the elevator door swished shut behind me.

Several stretchers, obviously in use, stood ominously between me and the door across the room, from which a light was shining. I glanced at the motionless gurneys and decided to risk it.

"Hello?" I called one more time, as I started toward the door.

No answer.

Swiftly, I moved across the cold floor, evading the sheet-covered corpses as effectively as possible. Just as I got to the end of the line of stretchers, directly in front of the door, the body beneath the sheet on the last gurney began to move!

"Eeeyahh!" I screamed.

The body sat up on the table.

"Oh! Ohhhoo," I cried, pushing toward the door. In my excitement, I smashed right into the gurney, as I tried to get by, causing the body to tumble to the floor. Then, I noticed that the "corpse" was not only moving, it was laughing! At me.

My friend threw the sheet off her shoulders and shrieked, "I gotcha, Abraham, I gotcha!"

"Gotcha?" I repeated. "You scared me nearly half to death!" Only then did it dawn on me that she may have been injured by the fall to the floor from the gurney. "Hey, are you okay?"

"Huh? Oh, yeah," she replied, as she allowed me to pull her to her feet.

"Wow, are you sure?" I asked. "I'm really sorry. I didn't mean to knock you for a loop."

"No problem," she answered perkily, as she dusted off her slacks. "After all," she continued, "everyone knows that dead men have no rights."

I'm not certain whether or not my friend's statement is true legally, but I know it is true spiritually. Dead men have no rights. Men and women who have been "crucified with Christ" have relinquished all claims to this world. They are "dead" to its allurements. They are "dead" to sin. They are "dead" to themselves. But they are vitally alive unto Christ.

When you surrender your rights to Jesus and submit to His leadership in your life, you may be tempted to regard your compliance as a negative transaction. For individuals who go no further, such is often the case. They confess and confess, surrender and surrender, but they never receive His power to live vigorously and victoriously a life of holiness.

If you want to experience positive holiness you must appropriate Christ's power. You must "put on" the Holy Spirit. As a "crucified" Christian, you have no rights of your own; but as you surrender to His Lordship, you have free access to all of the resources that are rightfully Christ's and are readily bestowed upon you by the Holy Spirit.

The big question is: "Whose side are you on?" Are you among those who are dying in sin, or those who are daily dying to sin and are vibrantly alive with Jesus?

Paul put it plainly, "That, in reference to your former

manner of life, you lay aside the old self, which is being corrupted in accordance with the lusts of deceit, and that you be renewed in the spirit of your mind, and put on the new self, which in the likeness of God has been created in righteousness and holiness of the truth" (Ephesians 4:22–24). As you take off the enemy's uniform, you put on the armor of God.

That doesn't mean that you will never have another problem, or that you will be supernaturally immune from tough times. Nor does it infer that you will never be tempted to take back your commitment. God will allow you to hold open that option until the day you die. It *does* mean that you are saying to God, "I am no longer concerned about the costs; no matter what the price tag, I want to belong totally to you."

When men and women are inducted into the United States' armed services, they take an oath of allegiance to their country. The ritual is rather perfunctory during times of peace, but when the country is at war, the pledge takes on profound significance.

Many who took the oath during the Vietnam War did not return. Others were captured and endured horrible humiliations as prisoners of war. They knew when they went to Vietnam that their lives were going to be endangered. They also understood, that at any point, they could go A.W.O.L., absent without leave. All the power of the United States government could not prevent a person from denying his or her country, from deserting his or her post, and disappearing into the dense jungles of Vietnam. But those soldiers had made a commitment. They had entered into an unconditional covenant that most of them would not compromise, even if it cost them their lives.

One P.O.W. shocked the world, when several years after the war was over, he was freed by the Vietnam government and returned home to America. As friends and family looked on, the fellow stepped off the plane, approached his commanding officer, saluted smartly, and said, "I'm reporting for new orders, sir."

That is commitment. And if a man can make that kind of unconditional pledge of loyalty to our country, how much more should a Christian be willing to make an irreversible, total surrender to the Lord Jesus Christ!

Is That All There Is?

When you are cleansed of sinful self-interest, and after you surrender the control of your life to Christ as completely as you can, that is not the end. That is the beginning!

An attractive woman in her mid-thirties approached me after I had spoken on this subject at her church. She came straight to the point. "I think I have allowed the Lord to cleanse me of all my sins. At least, I've confessed them often enough. And as far as I know, I have surrendered every area of my life to Christ. I've surrendered so many times that I know the words to "I Surrender All" by heart. And yet I feel that something is still missing. Am I filled with the Holy Spirit? Is that what holiness is all about?"

"I doubt it," I answered to both questions.

"Why not?" she sounded perplexed. "What else can I do? What more can God ask of me?"

"Nothing that I know of," I responded as kindly as possible.

She shifted uneasily as tears welled up in her eyes and slowly trickled down her face. "Then why am I not experiencing what you are calling 'positive holiness'? Why am I not living a Spirit-filled life? I want to. I've done all I can . . ." Her voice trailed off and the tears flowed freely now.

We sat down at the front of the church and I reviewed with her some of the Scriptures I have mentioned in this book. We talked about the cleansing of self-interest and the surrender of the control of her life to Christ.

"Have you done that?" I asked.

"Yes, but why am I still a spiritual failure?" she replied.

"Because the rest is not what God asks you to do; the rest is what the Holy Spirit does in and through you. It's hard to describe, but there is a point where God's demands upon you are satisfied, and if you have been obedient to Him, your responsibility goes no further. At that point, the Holy Spirit becomes obligated to you, and He does the work in you. Your part is to confess your sin, to allow Him to cleanse you; then surrender the controls of your life to Him. That is the negative part. The positive part takes place as you acknowledge Jesus as Lord in your life, and He begins to develop the fruit of the Spirit in you. At that point, it is not what you can do for Him; it is what He does in, for, and through you."

"What should I do then?" she implored.

"Nothing. Just accept His offer. Stand on His Word, and when the time is right, give testimony to your faith."

We prayed and she went home, skeptical, but hopeful.

Several months later, I was back in her town again, and she met me at the church door. She was radiant! Her countenance simply glowed with the love and joy of Christ.

"What happened to you?" I asked, as if I couldn't guess.

"He did it!" she bubbled. "He really did it! I took the Lord at His Word, and He took me at mine; and He filled me with His Holy Spirit."

Then she said something that struck me. "Wouldn't it have been awful," she said thoughtfully, "if I had done my part but had not allowed Him to do His?" Awful indeed.

How to Cause an Eternal Reflection

What will happen when you surrender the controls of your life to Christ? For one thing, your life will cast a positive reflection that will run all the way through eternity. The promise of Jesus to His disciples was that they would be "clothed with power from on high" (Luke 24:49) and that when the Holy Spirit had come upon them, they would receive power to be His witnesses (Acts 1:8). That's what happened to F. B. Meyer. After he was filled with the Holy Spirit, his contagious love of Jesus overflowed onto another young man who had a heart that was hungry for holiness. The young man's name was Oswald Chambers.

Oswald Chambers had committed his life to Christ as a boy. He was gifted in the areas of art and business, but the true thirsting of his soul was for the Word of God. He left the renowned Edinburgh University and poured himself into biblical studies at tiny Dunoon Bible Training College, where he became a tutor in philosophy.

While Chambers was at Dunoon, F. B. Meyer came to the school and spoke about the Holy Spirit. Meyer's words ignited a spark within Oswald that could not be quenched. Chambers wanted what F. B. Meyer had found. Although he wasn't quite sure what he was seeking, after listening to Meyer's glowing testimony, Oswald Chambers went immediately to his own room and asked God straightforwardly for the baptism of the Holy Spirit.

Nothing happened. That is, nothing as far as Oswald knew, but it was a beginning.

He later commented:

> From that day on for four years, nothing but the over-ruling grace of God and kindness of friends kept me out of an asylum.
>
> God used me during those years for the conversion of souls, but I had no conscious communion with Him. The Bible was the dullest, most uninteresting book in exist-ence, and the sense of depravity, the vileness and bad-motivedness of my nature, was terrific. . . .
>
> The last three months of those years things reached a climax, I was getting very desperate. I knew no one who had what I wanted; in fact I did not know what I did want. But I knew that if what I had was all the Christianity there was, the thing was a fraud. Then Luke 11:13 got hold of me—"If ye then, being evil, know how to give good gifts to your children, how much more shall your heavenly Father give the Holy Spirit to them that ask Him?"
>
> But how could I, bad-motivated as I was, possibly ask for the gift of the Holy Spirit? Then it was borne in upon me that I had to claim the gift from God on the authority of Jesus Christ and testify to having done so. But the thought came—if you claim the gift of the Holy Spirit on the word of Jesus Christ and testify to it, God will make it known to those who know you best how bad you are in heart. And I was not willing to be a fool for Christ's sake. But . . . I got to the place where I did not care whether everyone knew how bad I was; I cared for nothing on earth, saving to get out of my present condition.[1]

Oswald continued his quest for holiness, knowing all the while that he had already found the answer. He had but to appropriate the power and the presence of the Holy Spirit. He went to a mission meeting at Dunoon and knew that his time had come. He said, "I had no vision of God, only a sheer dogged determination to take God at His word and to prove this thing for myself, and I stood up and said so."

The woman who was in charge of the meeting knew Oswald Chambers well, and she assumed that such a spiritually devout fellow must have been inspired of the Lord to share a convicting word with the congregation. She told the group that Oswald had spoken as an example for the rest of them to follow.

But Chambers was not content to be confused as a spiritual giant when, in fact, he was seeking the fullness of God himself. "Up I got again and said: 'I got up for no one [else's] sake, I got up for my own sake; either Christianity is a downright fraud, or I have not got hold of the right end of the stick.' And then and there I claimed the gift of the Holy Spirit in dogged committal on Luke 11:33."

Still, nothing dramatic appeared to happen in Oswald's heart. But the next time he preached a sermon, forty people responded to his invitation to meet Christ. This terrified Chambers even more, so he went to his friend and spiritual mentor, Mr. MacGregor, and told him what had happened.

MacGregor kindly reminded Oswald of his public commitment. Chambers recalled: "He said, 'Don't you remember claiming the Holy Spirit as a gift on the word of Jesus, and that He said: "Ye shall receive power. . ."'? This is the power from on high.' Then like a flash something happened inside of me, and I saw that I had been wanting power in my own hand, so to speak, that I might say— Look what I have by putting my all on the altar."

Five years later, Oswald's heart was still overflowing with the fullness of God. He commented about his experience, "If the four previous years had been hell on earth, these five years have truly been heaven on earth. Glory be to God, the last aching abyss of the human heart is filled to overflowing with the love of God. Love is the beginning, love is the middle, and love is the end. After He comes in, all you see is 'Jesus only, Jesus ever.' "[2]

Oswald Chambers continued to grow deeper in his relationship with Christ. The Holy Spirit revealed to him many rare insights into spiritual truths through the Scripture, and Oswald passed along those revelations through his preaching, teaching, and writing. His classic devotional volume, *My Utmost for His Highest*, and the recently discovered *Devotions for a Deeper Life* describe his own rich walk with God while rewarding all who read them.

He died as a relatively young soldier in the British Army. This testimony was engraved upon his tombstone: "How much more will your heavenly Father give the Holy Spirit to them that ask Him?" (Luke 11:13.)

Are you filled with the Holy Spirit? Are you living in holiness? If not, ask Him to fill you right now. Your heavenly Father is true to His Word; He will do what He has promised.

13

More Power to You

The popular preacher was being hustled out of the church and through the noisy New York street, enroute to his next speaking engagement. Suddenly, a hand shot through the crowd of well-wishers and touched the preacher's shoulder. The preacher paused just long enough that the man who had touched him, an otherworldly-looking old man with white hair whipping in the wind, could capture his attention. With his finger pointing straight at the preacher, the elderly gentleman said, "Young man, when you speak again, honor the Holy Ghost."

The preacher was whisked away, but the words of the peculiar man continued ringing in his ears. To this day, nobody knows who that elderly stranger was or where he came from, but the preacher he pinned to the wall with his pointed words went on to become one of the world's most influential evangelists. His name was Dwight Lyman Moody.

The impression upon Moody was indelible. He later said, "I seldom stand before a great audience where I don't see that old man, with his outstretched finger, and hear his voice, 'Honor the Holy Ghost.' "

The stranger's words ignited a spark in Moody's heart, and God quickly fanned the flames. Back home in Chicago, Moody encountered two godly women, Mrs. Cooke and Mrs. Hawxhurst, members of his congregation. The two little ladies attended nearly all of Moody's meetings, always sitting in the front row. While the great pulpiteer was preaching, he could see that the women were praying. Each night, after the service had closed, the women would tell the speaker, "We have been praying for you."

"Why don't you pray for the people?" Mr. Moody would ask.

"Because you need the power of the Spirit," they would say.

Moody was honestly surprised by their assessment of his spiritual condition. His response, however, marked a turning point in his life:

> "I need the power! Why," said Mr. Moody, in relating the incident years after, "I thought I had power. I had the largest congregations in Chicago, and there were many conversions. I was in a sense satisfied. But right along those two godly women kept praying for me, and their earnest talk about anointing for special service set me to thinking. I asked them to come and talk with me, and they poured out their hearts in prayer that I might receive the filling of the Holy Spirit. There came a great hunger into my soul. I did not know what it was. I began to cry out as

I never did before. I really felt that I did not want to live if
I could not have this power for service."[1]

While Moody was attempting to understand the fire
within himself, another blaze broke out—the catastrophic
Chicago fire—which burned down over a third of the
"Windy City," including Mr. Moody's two churches. The
Moody family was forced to flee the flames with nothing
more than they could carry in a baby carriage.

With the scorched remains of his sanctuary still smol-
dering and sizzling in the cold, October drizzle, Moody
went back to New York to solicit funds from friends to
help rebuild the churches. He received money, but he
also found much more.

Moody said, "My heart was not in the work of begging.
I could not appeal. I was crying all the time that God
would fill me with His Spirit. Well, one day, in the city of
New York—oh, what a day!—I cannot describe it, I
seldom refer to it; it is almost too sacred an experience to
name. Paul had an experience of which he never spoke
for fourteen years. I can only say that God revealed
Himself to me, and I had such an experience of His love
that I had to ask Him to stay His hand."[2]

Even though D. L. Moody had difficulty describing his
encounter with the Holy, the results in his life and ministry
were dramatic. He said, "I went to preaching again. The
sermons were not different; I did not present any new
truths, and yet hundreds were converted. I would not now
be placed back where I was before that blessed experience
if you should give me all the world—."[3]

It may have been mere coincidence, or it might be
evidence of a divine sense of humor that the experience
that empowered Moody for world-changing service happened in the epicenter of man's economic wealth and

wisdom—Moody had been walking down Wall Street at the time. The evangelist was so overcome by the Holy Spirit that he went to the home of a friend in New York and requested a room where he could be alone with God. There the Spirit swept over him again in gigantic waves as Moody surrendered his sense of self-sufficiency to God. From that time on, D. L. Moody was a transformed man. Thousands of people met Jesus Christ through his preaching, and the ministry that bears his name still flourishes and reaches out to the world from downtown Chicago.

Moody's experience illustrates one of the most positive reasons why you need to seek out the fullness of God's Spirit: *that He may empower you to be the person He has called you to be.* Certainly, power without purity leads to corruption. But power with purity leads to spiritual renewal.

Who holds up revival in your town? Is it really the drunk or the drug-addict, the pervert, or the prostitute? No. God said, "[If] *My* people . . . humble themselves, and pray, and seek My face and turn from their wicked ways, then I will hear from heaven, will forgive their sin, and heal their land" (2 Chronicles 7:14, *italics mine*). Ironically, the wickedness of some Christians often thwarts the efforts of the Holy Spirit to transform sinful society.

Power to Witness

Perhaps one of the most powerful vehicles of revival the world has ever known began his ministry while still an unconverted choir director. Charles G. Finney was not a theologian, but a lawyer. His pastor, a Princeton graduate himself, asked the twenty-six-year-old attorney to lead the church choir. Finney liked the preacher and consented, though he readily admitted that he did not know Christ at the time.

Nevertheless, for the next three years, a group of young people banded together regularly to pray for Finney's conversion. Their efforts were not in vain. In between consultations with his law clients, Finney furtively began to read the Bible. Funny, before Finney began reading the Bible, he always had a copy lying on a table in his office. It lent integrity to the young attorney's business, although Finney himself never opened the Book. When he actually began *reading* the Bible, he became embarrassed and would quickly hide it when a client came in. According to his biographer, Basil Miller, if someone dropped by unexpectedly, catching him in the act, Finney "carelessly threw law books over the Bible, 'to create the impression that I had not had it in hand.' "[4]

The Spirit of the Book, however, grabbed Finney's heart. One day, Finney left his law office and went out into the woods to pray, determined that he would not return until he had either given his heart to God or died in the attempt. He prayed from early morning until well past noon, and God found Finney.

Later that night, alone in his law office once again, the Spirit of God came upon him. Finney's testimony of what happened next is astounding:

> I closed the door and turned around, my heart seemed to be liquid within me. All of my feelings seemed to rise and flow out; and the utterance of my heart was, "I want to pour my whole soul out to God." The rising of my soul was so great that I rushed into the room back of the front office, to pray. There was no fire, and no light, in the room; nevertheless it appeared to me as if it were perfectly light. As I went in and shut the door after me, it seemed as if I

met the Lord Jesus Christ face to face. It did not occur to
me then, nor did it for some time afterward, that it was
wholly a mental state. On the contrary, it seemed to me
that I saw him as I would see any other man. He said
nothing, but looked at me in such a manner as to break me
right down at his feet . . . it seemed to me a reality, that he
stood before me, and I fell down at his feet and poured out
my soul to him. I wept aloud like a child, and made such
confessions as I could with my choked utterance. It
seemed to me that I bathed his feet with my tears; and yet
I had no distinct impression that I touched him. . . .

I returned to the front office, and found that the fire that
I had made of large wood was nearly burned out. But as I
turned and was about to take a seat by the fire, I received
a mighty baptism of the Holy Ghost. Without any expec-
tation of it, without ever having the thought in my mind
that there was any such thing for me, without any recol-
lection that I had ever heard the thing mentioned by any
person in the world, the Holy Spirit descended upon me
in a manner that seemed to go through me, body and soul.
I could feel the impression, like a wave of electricity,
going through and through me. Indeed it seemed to come
in waves and waves of liquid love; for I could not express
it in any other way. It seemed like the very breath of
God. . . . No words can express the wonderful love that
was shed abroad in my heart. I wept aloud with joy and
love; and I do not know but I should say, I literally
bellowed out the unutterable gushings of my heart. These
waves came over me, and over me, and over me, one after
the other, until I recollect I cried out, "I shall die if these
waves continue to pass over me." I said, "Lord, I can not
bear any more"; yet I had no fear of death.[5]

It is interesting to note that Finney did not need to be
coached, coerced, or cajoled into receiving the fullness of
the Holy Spirit. He admitted that he had not even known

that such an experience existed. He was a lawyer, not a Bible scholar. Though he later became a great student of the Bible, his theological understanding and some of his teachings remained suspect. His *Systematic Theology* is still disputed by many biblical scholars. Nevertheless, as Harold Lindsell commented in *The Holy Spirit in the Latter Days,* "Whatever he had, we all need."[6]

Charles Finney became the living embodiment of the verse "But you shall receive power when the Holy Spirit has come upon you; and you shall be My witnesses . . ." (Acts 1:8). After he was filled with the Spirit, Finney became a fiery and effective witness for Christ. Almost immediately, he sparked a spiritual renewal within his own church and among his companions. Nearly all of his former, profligate friends came to know Christ through Finney's influence. Often, he would speak only a few words but the Spirit of God used them as a jackhammer to crush a person's heart with conviction over sin. Whole congregations and entire communities were literally transformed as God used Finney to inspire spiritual revival both in America and Europe.

As could be expected, the enthusiastic evangelist encountered extreme opposition and severe criticism. Preachers railed against him and rebuked him as a rabble-rouser rather than a revivalist. In more than one town, his image was burned in effigy as crowds of Christians screamed in delight.

Strangely, many of the accusations for which Finney was sorely castigated are now common practices among evangelical Christians. He was criticized for publicizing his evangelistic crusades; he was rebuffed for preaching long, harsh sermons and for allowing women to pray in public. He was soundly denounced for asking people to "come forward" and make a public declaration of their faith. When individuals wished to inquire further about their salvation, he often set aside a separate room for this purpose. Sometimes, he would designate a special seat for inquirers, which quickly came to be known as the "anxious seat," for obvious reasons. These practices, too, were condemned by churchmen and pagans alike, who did not appreciate "religion" being so personal.

Despite mammoth opposition, Charles Finney continued to proclaim the message of full salvation for more than fifty years. He was personally responsible for the conversion of at least half a million people during his lifetime, and his writings continue to rend hearts and rekindle revival yet today. Unquestionably, Finney, himself, and Church historians would trace the secret of his success to his experience of being filled with the Holy Spirit.

Similarly, if you hope to impact secular society, you will need the power of the Holy Spirit in your life. If you are going to win your non-Christian friends and family to Jesus Christ, they need to be able to see the products of holiness in you—a peace, poise, purity, and power—that unbelievers simply do not have.

Hundreds of witnesses could be called at this point to emphasize this vital, intimate link between holiness and effective Christian service. For example, Asa Mahon, the president of Oberlin College, where Finney taught and popularized his views, stressed that holiness and spiritual power cannot be separated. To Mahon, the baptism of the Holy Spirit produced two primary results in a person's life: power to live in a godly manner and power to witness effectively for Christ. Sadly, many twentieth-century Christians have attempted to separate these two.

R. A. Torrey, an associate of D. L. Moody, emphasized

that effective evangelism must be empowered by the Spirit. So did A. J. Gordon and A. B. Simpson. Another person who clearly connected the Spirit's power with holy living was the president of what was to become Princeton University, Jonathan Edwards. So also did Charles Haddon Spurgeon, A. W. Tozer, William Law, John Owen, Samuel Chadwick, and the famous mathematician, Blaise Pascal.

In fact, you would be hard-pressed to find a true saint who has not attributed his or her spiritual power to the overflowing presence of the Holy Spirit. If you think about it, that only makes sense. After all, what can a person really do for God without the power of the Holy Spirit? It is impossible to be holy unless the Holy One is within you. Similarly, it is only by the supernatural presence of His Spirit that you can do His superhuman work. To express effectively Christ's personality in the world, you need His presence and His power—you need the Spirit of Holiness.

Power to Accept Yourself

Practical reasons for pursuing a life of holiness abound, but perhaps the most basic ones have to do with your personality and conduct. Simply stated, holiness will probably improve both. Please don't misunderstand. Holiness does not normally change your psychological personality type. If you are a hyperactive, "type A" personality, you will probably remain so even though you are holy. The Apostle Paul did. Similarly, if you are an introvert before becoming holy, it is highly unlikely that the Holy Spirit will suddenly transform you into an extrovert.

How then does holiness improve your personality? By

integrating it around the Person of Jesus Christ. Let me explain. When you surrender completely to the Lordship of Christ, He brings a sense of personal unity and unified purpose into your life. Have you ever met someone who seems to be constantly disoriented, confused, running to and fro but hardly ever accomplishing anything? They say, "My life is coming apart at the seams." They are *disintegrated*. To be *integrated* means that your life is being pulled back together. Jesus does that in you, putting everything into proper perspective, and giving you a positive purpose to live, a reason to face another day—to spend time with Him and to present Christ to the world. This spills over into your sense of self-worth and self-respect. Because you know you belong to Christ and are accepted by Him, you exude a kind of confidence that is impossible to achieve through Christless self-improvement programs. Of course, being cleansed of sin, forgiven, and freed of past guilt and shame does wonders for your personality, too!

Holy people rarely put themselves down, nor do they exalt themselves. Their self-images are secure in Christ and not dependent upon the opinions or thoughts of other people. As such, holy people are free from the tyranny of always trying to impress somebody.

Furthermore, when your personality is orientated around Christ's character, you become more consistent in your other personal relationships. Why? Because it is "Christ in you" who is at work, constantly refining you into the person He created you to be. And Christ's character is consistent. He will produce a similar poise and stability in you with regard to your relationships to other people. Of course, you may still express strong opinions or emotions. But when someone contradicts or disagrees with your opinion, or takes advantage of you emotionally, you are able to deal with those tensions in a Christ-like manner, without becoming bitter, jealous, or antagonistic. The same consistency will be evident in your ability to handle trials, testings, and temptations.

Undoubtedly, rejection is one of the main reasons for many personality problems. Myriads of people suffer a sense of self-rejection, which usually results in further rejection by others. Some may attempt to conceal this personal humiliation by rationalizing—convincing themselves that the problem lies with somebody or everybody else. Others overcompensate for their lack of self-esteem, as is often the case with the loud, boisterous, blowhard type of person. Wimps and whiners cover their deficient feelings about themselves by constantly putting themselves down. Still others turn to drugs, alcohol, or sexual promiscuity in their search for acceptance.

The holy person knows that he or she has been cleansed of sin and accepted by God. Therefore, self-acceptance becomes only logical, though it is not always easy. Still, who are you to argue with God? If He accepts you, you can accept yourself! Otherwise, you are insulting His holiness.

Power to Serve

Something marvelous happens when a saint discovers that self-acceptance is consistent with holiness. Suddenly, he or she is willing and *able* to give himself or herself away in the service of Christ, and in self-effacing service to other people. No longer is it necessary to protect one's image before the public; to make sure you are seen "in all the right places, with all the right people." (Can you imagine Mother Teresa of Calcutta worrying about her image?) When you are holy, you can fearlessly pour yourself into the most magnificent or the most menial task, knowing full well that your worth is not determined by the job you do or your station in life, but by who you are in Christ Jesus.

Jesus declared, "No one can serve two masters; for either he will hate the one and love the other, or he will hold to one and despise the other. You cannot serve God and mammon" (Matthew 6:24). Most of us assume that Jesus was talking only about the perils of money. Not so! The key word in that last phrase is not *mammon*; it is *and*. You can't serve God *and* . . . anything. Only when you are exclusively His are you ready to serve others.

It is the holy person, the one who has been delivered from the tyranny of self-interest and is "crucified with Christ," whose head and heart are "together," who is best able to unselfishly serve other people. The holy person can serve without a selfish motive, without concern for what he or she is going to get out of serving, because his or her service is what Jesus would do.

That principle—"What would Jesus do?"—governs the conduct of a holy person. It is a simple guide by which a holy individual can check every action. Would Jesus express Himself in that manner? Would Jesus approve of that type of dress? Would He go to that place? How would He deal with this particular business situation? How would He do this job? What would be His ethical response in this specific circumstance?

The principle is poignantly portrayed by Charles M. Sheldon in his classic work *In His Steps*. Sheldon shows holiness in action by taking his characters through a series of conflicts in their lives. The characters attempt to solve their ethical dilemmas by asking the simple question: "What would Jesus do?" and then *doing* it.

Many of those who responded positively in obedience

to what they felt Jesus would do were blessed beyond measure as a result. Although, in stark contrast to the "health, wealth, and prosperity" doctrines that have gained popularity in the latter part of the twentieth century, some of Sheldon's characters obeyed the Holy Spirit, did what they thought Jesus would do, and *still* suffered dire consequences. Regardless of their circumstances, Sheldon's characters served Christ and mankind, not so they could be blessed, but so they could be a means of blessing.

Power to Love

If holiness promises anything, it provides the power whereby you can love with Christ's supernatural love. A holy person's life is characterized by love—love for God, certainly, but also love for one another. This was the one true badge of holy living as far as Jesus was concerned. The night before His crucifixion He exhorted His disciples, "A new commandment I give to you, that you love one another, even as I have loved you, that you also love one another. By this all men will know that you are My disciples, if you have love for one another" (John 13:34, 35).

Notice, Jesus did not say that the sign of true Christianity is a cross worn about your neck. Nor did He say anything about church attendance, communion, or putting money in the offering plate. He said, "My disciples will be distinguished by their love."

Holy love is not merely mushy, gushy, syrupy sentiment. It is *tough* love. It is *sacrificial* love. It is *unconditional* love. It is *giving* love. It is *Christ-like* love. Certainly, this is the quality of love Paul was depicting in his eloquent declaration in 1 Corinthians 13. To the holy person, this manifesto of love is no lofty ideal. It is the way God desires His children to live.

What is holy love like? Paul says that this kind of love "is patient, love is kind, and is not jealous; love does not brag and is not arrogant, does not act unbecomingly; it does not seek its own, is not provoked, does not take into account a wrong suffered, does not rejoice in unrighteousness, but rejoices with the truth; bears all things, believes all things, hopes all things, endures all things" (1 Corinthians 13:4–7).

"Whoa! Wait a minute!" you may be saying. "That's totally unrealistic. How am I supposed to love that way?"

You can't. Not on your own power, at least. Nevertheless, the grand privilege and obligation of the holy person is that Christ can fill your heart so full of His holy love, you won't be able to contain it all. It was an explosion of this love in the heart of Samuel Logan Brengle that launched him into a life of holiness.

In his book *When the Holy Ghost Is Come*, Brengle described his experience:

I had been searching the Scriptures, ransacking my heart, humbling my soul, and crying to God almost day and night for a pure heart and the baptism with the Holy Ghost, when one glad, sweet day (it was January 9, 1885) this text suddenly opened to my understanding: "If we confess our sins, He is faithful and just to forgive our sins, and to cleanse us from all unrighteousness"; and I was enabled to believe without any doubt that the precious Blood cleansed my heart, even mine, from all sin. Shortly after that, while reading these words of Jesus to Martha: "I am the resurrection and the life; he that believeth in Me, though he were dead, yet shall he live: And whosoever liveth and believeth in Me shall never never die" (John 11:25, 26)—instantly my heart was melted like wax before

fire; Jesus Christ was revealed to my spiritual consciousness, revealed in me, and my soul was filled with unutterable love. I walked in a heaven of love. Then one day,
with amazement, I said to a friend: "This is the perfect
love about which the Apostle John wrote; but it is beyond
all I dreamed of. In it is personality. This love thinks,
wills, talks with me, corrects me, instructs and teaches
me." And then I knew that God the Holy Ghost was in this
love and this love was God, for "God is love."[7]

A few days following this revelation, Brengle was
scheduled to speak at a church in Boston. At the close of
his message, he included a personal testimony in which
he stated categorically that God had cleansed his heart of
sin. "That confession," Brengle later wrote in the introduction to Helps to Holiness, "put me on record." It also
opened the windows of heaven to Brengle. He described
the results in Helps to Holiness:

Two mornings after that, just as I got out of bed and was
reading some of the words of Jesus, He gave me such a
blessing as I never had dreamed a man could have this
side of Heaven. It was a heaven of love that came into my
heart. I walked out over Boston Common before breakfast
weeping for joy and praising God. Oh, how I loved! In that
hour I knew Jesus and I loved Him till it seemed my heart
would break with love. I loved the sparrows, I loved the
dogs, I loved the horses, I loved the little urchins on the
streets, I loved the strangers who hurried past me, I loved
the heathen—I loved the whole world.[8]

Then, as though he could not contain the words any
longer, Samuel Logan Brengle penned a beautiful defini-
tion of positive holiness. The saintly Salvationist said:

Do you want to know what holiness is? It is pure love. Do you want to know what the baptism of the Holy Ghost is? It is not mere sentiment. It is not a happy sensation that passes away in a night. It is a baptism of love that brings every thought into captivity to the Lord Jesus (2 Corinthians 10:5); that casts out all fear (1 John 4:18); that burns up doubt and unbelief as fire burns tow; that makes one "meek and lowly in heart" (Matthew 11:29); that makes one hate uncleanness, lying and deceit, a flattering tongue and every evil way with a perfect hatred; that makes Heaven and Hell eternal realities; that makes one patient and gentle with the froward and sinful; that makes one "pure, . . . peaceable, . . . easy to be entreated, full of mercy and good fruits, without partiality, and without hypocrisy" (James 3:17); that brings one into perfect and unbroken sympathy with the Lord Jesus Christ in His toil and travail to bring a lost and rebel world back to God. God did all that for me, bless His holy name![9]

God will do all that, and more, in you when you allow Him to make you holy.

14

How Can You Be Holy?

Throughout these pages, I have tenaciously fought the temptation to spell out a formula for transforming you into a holy person. I am well aware that others have spelled out such "how-to" steps to spirituality, but I have purposely avoided a "one-size-fits-all" recipe for holiness simply because God is so incredibly imaginative, creative, and unpredictable (in a positive sense!) in the ways He works in people's lives. If you examine the Scripture passages that the Spirit has employed to press saints of the past into holiness, you will marvel at the amazing diversity. That ought to indicate something to us. Namely, that God works His wonders in each of our lives in *different* ways!

With that disclaimer (and as a concession to my disdain for authors and speakers who have a penchant for preaching about *what* we should do, but never seem to get around to telling us *how* to do it), here are four simple steps to holiness. (Okay, okay . . . I just couldn't resist!)

First, *believe that God can make you holy here and now.* Many devout Christians hope to become holy someday, if not here on earth, hopefully in heaven. But the Spirit of God impressed Peter in those first few years after Pentecost to exhort us: "Be holy yourselves also in all your behavior; because it is written, 'You shall be holy, for I am holy.' . . . conduct yourselves in fear [holy, reverential awe] *during the time of your stay upon earth* . . ." (1 Peter 1:15–17, *italics mine*). Clearly, Peter is implying that holiness is something to be pursued in *this* lifetime, not simply in the life to come.

John Wesley often asked his audiences such penetrating questions as:

1. Have you received the Holy Spirit's fullness since you have believed?
2. Will you ever need Him more than you do right now?
3. Will you ever be "more ready" to receive Him than right now?
4. Will God ever be "more ready" to fill you with His Holy Spirit than He is right now?

If you answered no to any of the above questions, then begin your quest for holiness by believing that God can deliver you from the bondage of sin; He can cleanse your heart, mind, and mouth; and He can fill you with His Holy Presence—right now.

It is strange to study how unsaved individuals will struggle so strongly to avoid meeting Jesus Christ. Perhaps that is understandable, since they are caught in the stubborn, unrelenting squeeze of sin in their lives. What is difficult to understand is why a person who knows Jesus Christ should ever avoid allowing Him to have full control. If you know the Lord, you can be sure that His will for you is good; He wants only the best for you. You can trust Him; believe Him for His best right now.

Second, *completely renounce all known sin in your life.* If you are unholy, admit it. Confess your need and your desire to be clean before your Lord. This step is crucial, because if the Holy Spirit is revealing an area of sin in your life and you refuse to repent of it, your spiritual progress will stall at that point until you are willing to allow Him to cleanse you. If you are unsure of which sin is blocking the flow of His Spirit in your life, pray something such as this: "Lord, please convict me of my sinfulness." Then, watch out—it may be the most rapid response to prayer you ever receive!

Are you reticent to give up your sin? Risk it. Frankly, you can always return to your filth if you find that you are not satisfied with Christ; the devil will always be glad to take you back. On the other hand, once you experience Christ, in the beauty of holiness, you most likely will never want to be stained by sin again.

As a youngster, my favorite playgrounds were the mounds of black, bituminous coal slag that rose all around our Pennsylvania town. After a delightful day in the coal dust, I would trudge home, deviously trying to devise some method by which I could avoid taking a bath. I was filthy and proud of it! Normally, my parents had to beg, threaten, or trick me into the tub.

Then, one day I discovered girls. Suddenly, being clean seemed so exciting! I never wanted to be dirty again. Something similar happens when you discover how beautiful life with Christ can be. Sin will lose its fatal attraction.

Third, *surrender completely every area of your life to the Lordship of Christ.* Hold nothing back. Give Him all the keys. There's no time for hypocrisy now. You cannot attempt to bargain with God ("I'll give you this area, God, if You will give me that gift") if you hope to enter into holiness. As you obey Christ and allow Him to have absolute control in your life, He will fill you with His Spirit. He will then continue to expand your capacity to be filled for the rest of your life, producing more and more of His character—the fruit of the Spirit—in you.

This is a never-ending process. You can never plumb the depths of God's love. You will never exhaust His fresh supply of resources in your life. There is no height, nor depth, no limit at all to how deeply you can grow in Christ. His Spirit will continue to extend your horizons.

Maybe that explains why truly holy people rarely become bored. Just about the time you say, "Okay, God, I think I've got a handle on this Christian life; I think I've gone as far as I can go," He says, "Oh, really? Well, open wide, because I'm going to do something more in your heart, something your mind has not even yet conceived!" What an exciting way to live! And it begins the moment you wholeheartedly place your life in His hands.

William Booth, the founder of the Salvation Army, was often asked the secret to his spiritual success. In his later years, the great General would respond, "The secret of my success is that God had all there was of William Booth."[1]

Finally, *simply trust the Lord, with childlike faith, to fill you with His Holy Spirit and to empower you to live in holiness.* Remember, He is the One who does this in you; holiness is not something you do for Him. Allow Him the freedom to bring about the results of holiness in your life. You needn't try to conjure up the fruit or the gifts of the Spirit. The promise of Jesus is, "If you then, being evil, know how to give good gifts to your children, how much more shall your heavenly Father give the Holy Spirit to those who ask Him?" (Luke 11:13). The parallel passage in Matthew puts it this way: "How much more shall your Father who is in heaven give what is good to those who ask Him!" (Matthew 7:11). What greater gift could God give you than Himself?

This glorious transaction—yourself for Himself—is what Hudson Taylor humbly referred to as "the exchanged life." Six months after the dedicated missionary wrote that despairing letter to his mother (which I discussed earlier), Mr. Taylor received an encouraging note from his friend, Mr. McCarthy. God used a simple paragraph in McCarthy's letter to lead Hudson Taylor into holiness, or the exchanged life. In the book *Hudson Taylor's Spiritual Secret*, his biographers included a letter to his sister describing his discovery:

> The last month or more has been, perhaps, the happiest of my life, and I long to tell you a little of what the Lord has done for my soul. . . .
>
> Perhaps I may make myself more clear if I go back a little. Well, dearie, my mind has been greatly exercised for six or eight months past, feeling the need personally and for our Mission of more holiness, life, power in our souls. But personal need stood first and was the greatest. I felt the ingratitude, the danger, the sin of not living nearer to God. I prayed, fasted, strove, made resolutions, read the Word more diligently, sought more time for meditation— but all without avail. Every day, almost every hour, the consciousness of sin oppressed me. . . .
>
> Then came the question, is there no rescue? Must it be thus to the end—constant conflict, and too often defeat? How could I preach with sincerity that, to those who receive Jesus, "to them gave He power to become the sons

of God" (i.e., Godlike) when it was not so in my own
experience? Instead of growing stronger, I seemed to be
getting weaker and to have less power against sin; and no
wonder, for faith and even hope were getting low. I hated
myself, I hated my sin, yet gained no strength against it. I
felt I *was* a child of God. . . . But to rise to my privileges as
a child, I was utterly powerless.[2]

It is important to note that Hudson Taylor felt absolutely certain that he was a Christian. Yet he knew there
had to be more to the Christian life than the level of
frustration that he was experiencing. He had heard about
holiness but remained confused. He continues:

I thought that holiness, practical holiness, was to be
gradually attained by a diligent use of the means of grace.
There was nothing I so much desired as holiness, nothing
I so much needed; but far from in any measure attaining it,
the more I strove after it, the more it eluded my grasp,
until hope itself almost died out, and I began to think
that—perhaps to make heaven the sweeter—God would
not give it down here. I do not think that I was striving to
attain it in my own strength. I knew I was powerless. . . .

And yet, never did Christ seem more precious; a Saviour
who could and would save such a sinner! . . . And
sometimes there were seasons not only of peace but of joy
in the Lord; but they were transitory, and at best there was
a sad lack of power. . . .

All the time I felt assured that there was in Christ all I
needed, but the practical question was—how to get it out.
He was rich truly, but I was poor; He was strong, but I
weak. . . . As gradually as light dawned, I saw that faith
was the only requisite—was the hand to lay hold on His
fulness and make it mine. But I had not this faith.

I strove for faith, but it would not come; I tried to exercise it, but in vain. . . . I prayed for faith, but it came not. What was I to do?[3]

Just as Hudson Taylor was about to give up all hope of ever being holy, he received Mr. McCarthy's simple, but earth-shaking revelation. Taylor recalled:

McCarthy, who had been much exercised by the same sense of failure but saw the light before I did, wrote (I quote from memory):

"But how to get faith strengthened? Not by striving after faith, but by resting on the Faithful One."

As I read, I saw it all!. . . I looked to Jesus and saw (and when I saw, oh, how joy flowed!) that He said, "I will never leave thee."

"Ah, there is rest!" I thought. "I have striven in vain to rest in Him. I'll strive no more. . . ." As I thought of the Vine and the branches, what light the blessed Spirit poured direct into my soul! How great seemed my mistake in wishing to get the sap, the fulness out of Him! I saw not only that Jesus will never leave me, but that I am a member of His body, of His flesh and of His bones. . . .

Oh, my dear Sister, it is a wonderful thing to be really one with a risen and exalted Saviour, to be a member of Christ! Think what it involves. Can Christ be rich and I poor? Can your right hand be rich and your left poor? or your head be well fed while your body starves? Again, think of its bearing on prayer. . . . No more can your prayers or mine be discredited if offered in the name of Jesus (i.e., not for the sake of Jesus merely, but on the ground that we are His, His members) so long as we keep within the limits of Christ's credit—a tolerably wide limit![4]

Hudson Taylor had discovered the secret to spiritual success: It was resting in the knowledge that Christ was in him and he was "in Christ." With overflowing joy, he gushed concerning the peace he had found:

> The sweetest part, if one may speak of one part being sweeter than another, is the rest which full identification with Christ brings. I am no longer anxious about anything, as I realize this; for He, I know, is able to carry out His will, and His will is mine. It makes no matter where He places me, or how. That is rather for Him to consider than for me; for in the easiest position He must give me His grace, and in the most difficult His grace is sufficient. . . .
> And since Christ has thus dwelt in my heart by faith, how happy I have been!. . . I am no better than before. In a sense, I do not wish to be, nor am I striving to be. But I am dead and buried with Christ—and risen too! And now Christ lives in me, and "the life that I now live in the flesh, I live by the faith of the Son of God, who loved me and gave himself for me. . . ."[5]

In concluding his letter, Hudson Taylor, always concerned for the spiritual welfare of others, exhorted his sister to find the secret of Christ's fullness for herself. Allow his words to encourage you, as well:

> May God give you to lay hold on these blessed truths. . . . do not let us consider Him as far off, when God has made us one with Him, members of His very body. Nor should we look upon this experience, these truths, as for a few. They are the birthright of every child of God, and no one can dispense with them without dishonouring our Lord. The only power for deliverance from sin or for true service is Christ.[6]

The life-style that Hudson Taylor experienced is what I
have called "positive holiness." His life became saturated
with "love, joy, peace, patience, kindness, goodness,
faithfulness, gentleness, self-control"—the fruit of the
Spirit, the character of Jesus Christ *alive* in him. His
secret to victorious living was simply Christ—Christ in
His fullness.

That's what the Apostle Peter felt inspired to express
fervently from that tiny hideaway in first-century Rome.
Perhaps he thought even then that his days were num-
bered. If so, he was right.

Within three years, the demented mind of the despot
emperor Nero darkened still further. He expressed his
insanity by violently victimizing innocent followers of
"The Way," as Christianity was called. Many Christians
were maligned publicly. Others were decapitated, crucified, or cruelly tortured in unfair, one-sided "contests" in
the Roman Colosseum.

Peter knew that he would soon be picked up by Nero's
police and placed under arrest. When that happened, the
Apostle's life would be over. He had heard that Paul was
traveling toward Rome. Possibly, his co-worker had arrived already; it was so difficult to get accurate information these days, now that the Christians had been forced
to meet in the catacombs and sewers beneath the city.

Perhaps, thought Peter, *if Paul comes, maybe he can
carry on the work here.* That was some comfort. Still,
Peter felt he must get one final letter out to those who had
believed in Christ because of him. He was alone now—
Silas had gone to work with Paul—so Peter sat down to
pen the message himself.

In a dark, dank corner of the catacombs, lighted only by
a small candle, the Apostle thought back to some of the
last words Jesus had spoken to him after the Resurrection,

not long before the Master had ascended into heaven. *What was it that He had said?* Peter tried to recall. *Oh, yes. I remember now. He said, "Truly, truly, I say to you, when you were younger, you used to gird yourself, and walk wherever you wished; but when you grow old, you will stretch out your hands, and someone else will gird you, and bring you where you do not wish to go"* (John 21:18).

At the time Jesus had said that, Peter was confused. He couldn't comprehend the meaning of Christ's words. Now, as he picked up his pen, he understood that Jesus had been predicting Peter's own death. The Apostle took a deep breath and exhaled slowly before beginning to scribble rapidly upon the parchment:

I consider it right, as long as I am in this earthly dwelling, to stir you up by way of reminder, knowing that the laying aside of my earthly dwelling is imminent, as also our Lord Jesus Christ has made clear to me. And I will also be diligent that at any time after my departure you may be able to call these things to mind.

                                                    2 Peter 1:13–15

The Apostle then went on to encourage the saints, many of whom were already experiencing intense persecution. "Don't give up," Peter told them. "Keep applying all diligence; continue pursuing moral excellence; keep persevering! Things may get a little rough and rocky, but don't despair. Jesus is coming! Keep looking for the Second Coming of the Lord Jesus. Don't get discouraged because He hasn't come yet—a thousand years as are one day to our Lord—but continue to live in expectancy, in peace, and in holiness."

Finally, the tired but triumphant Apostle wrote: "But the day of the Lord will come like a thief, in which the heavens will pass away with a roar and the elements will be destroyed with intense heat, and the earth and its works will be burned up" (2 Peter 3:10). Peter paused to ponder the ramifications of the prophetic words he had penned. *What should they do then? How should they live?* The answer was obvious. He began to pour out his heart onto the page: "Since all these things are to be destroyed in this way, what sort of people ought you to be . . ."

"Holy!" Peter's heart cried out. "*Holy!* That's the kind of people you ought to be!"

He continued writing: ". . . in holy conduct and godliness, looking for and hastening the coming of the day of God. . . . Therefore, beloved, since you look for these things, be diligent to be found by Him in peace, spotless and blameless. . . . but grow in the grace and knowledge of our Lord and Savior Jesus Christ. To Him be the glory, both now and to the day of eternity. Amen" (2 Peter 3:11, 12, 14, 18).

Holiness. *Positive holiness.* It was possible for Peter. It was practical for Paul. And for Hudson Taylor, and Samuel Logan Brengle. It marked the lives of Finney, Moody, and a host of others.

May positive holiness be the prevailing testimony of your life . . . until Jesus comes!

Source Notes

Chapter 1
1. Jerry Bridges, *The Pursuit of Holiness* (Colorado Springs: Navpress, 1978), p. 33.
2. J. C. Ryle, *Holiness* (Old Tappan, N.J.: Fleming H. Revell Company, n.d.), p. 19.

Chapter 2
1. James Gilchrist Lawson, *Deeper Experiences of Famous Christians* (Anderson, Ind.: Warner Press, 1911), p. 253.
2. Ibid., pp. 255–56.
3. Edith Dean, *Great Women of the Christian Faith* (New York: Harper & Row, Publishers, 1959; reprint ed., Westwood, N.J.: Barbour and Company), p. 220.
4. Ibid., p. 221.

Chapter 3
1. Helen Roseveare, *Living Holiness* (Minneapolis: Bethany House Publishers, 1986), p. 43.

Chapter 4
1. James Gilchrist Lawson, *Deeper Experiences of Famous Christians* (Anderson, Ind.: Warner Press, 1911), pp. 264–65.
2. The Rev. N. Burwash, *Wesley's 52 Sermons* (Salem, Ohio: Convention Book Store, 1967), p. 392.

Chapter 5
1. Thomas H. Darlow, *Frances Ridley Havergal* (Old Tappan, N.J.: Fleming H. Revell Company, 1927), p. 34.
2. Maria V. G. Havergal, *Memorials of Frances Ridley Havergal by Her Sister* (New York: Anson D. R. Randolph and Company, 1880).
3. Donald S. Metz, *Studies in Biblical Holiness* (Kansas City, Mo.: Beacon Hill Press, 1971), p. 205.
4. V. Raymond Edman, *They Found the Secret*, Clarion Classics edition (Grand Rapids, Mich.: Zondervan Publishing House, 1984), pp. 127–28.
5. Ibid., p. 129.
6. Ibid., p. 130.
7. Andrew Murray, *The Believer's Secret of Holiness* (Minneapolis: Bethany House Publishers, 1984), p. 158.

Chapter 6
1. Jerry Bridges, *The Pursuit of Holiness* (Colorado Springs: Navpress, 1978), p. 20.
2. Ibid., p. 21.
3. Ibid., p. 84.

Chapter 7
1. V. Raymond Edman, *They Found the Secret*, Clarion Classics edition (Grand Rapids, Mich.: Zondervan Publishing House, 1984), p. 10.
2. Norman Vincent Peale, *The Positive Power of Jesus Christ* (Wheaton, Ill.: Tyndale House Publishers, 1980), pp. 50–52.
3. Ibid.
4. Armando Valladares, *Against All Hope* (New York: Ballantine Books, 1986), pp. 255–56.
5. Ibid., pp. 257–58.

Chapter 8
1. R. C. Sproul, *The Holiness of God* (Wheaton, Ill.: Tyndale House Publishers, 1985), pp. 123–24.

2. Roland Bainton, *Here I Stand* (New York: New American Library, Mentor Books, 1978), pp. 49–50.
3. A. B. Simpson, *Days of Heaven on Earth: A Daily Devotional*, Francis Asbury Press edition (Camp Hill, Pa.: Christian Publications, 1984), January 7.
4. Dr. and Mrs. Howard Taylor, *Hudson Taylor's Spiritual Secret* (Chicago: Moody Press, 1932), pp. 152–53.
5. Ibid.
6. Ibid.
7. Ibid.

Chapter 9
1. Norman Grubb, *C. T. Studd* (Fort Washington, Pa.: Christian Literature Crusade, 1974), p. 36.
2. Ibid., p. 38.
3. Ibid.
4. Ibid., p. 39.

Chapter 11
1. Harold Lindsell, *The Holy Spirit in the Latter Days* (Nashville, Tenn.: Thomas Nelson, Inc., 1983), p. 140.
2. E. Stanley Jones, *A Song of Ascents* (Nashville, Tenn.: Abingdon Press, 1968), p. 51.
3. Ibid., p. 52.
4. Ibid., p. 53.
5. Ibid., p. 55.

Chapter 12
1. V. Raymond Edman, *They Found the Secret*, Clarion Classics edition (Grand Rapids, Mich.: Zondervan Publishing House, 1984), p. 33.
2. Ibid., p. 34.

Chapter 13
1. William R. Moody, *The Life of Dwight L. Moody* (Old Tappan, N. J.: Fleming H. Revell Company, 1900), pp. 146–47.
2. Ibid., p. 149.
3. Ibid.
4. Basil Miller, *Charles Finney* (Minneapolis: Bethany Fellowship, 1961), p. 19.
5. Charles G. Finney, *An Autobiography* (Old Tappan, N.J.: Fleming H. Revell Company, 1908), pp. 19–21.
6. Harold Lindsell, *The Holy Spirit in the Latter Days* (Nashville, Tenn.: Thomas Nelson, Inc., 1983), p. 133.
7. S. L. Brengle, *When the Holy Ghost Is Come* (Atlanta: The Salvation Army, 1976), pp. 7–8.
8. S. L. Brengle, *Helps to Holiness* (London: Salvationist Publishing, 1948), introduction.
9. Ibid.

Chapter 14
1. John D. Waldon, *The Privilege of All Believers* (Atlanta: The Salvation Army), p. 104.
2. Dr. and Mrs. Howard Taylor, *Hudson Taylor's Spiritual Secret* (Chicago: Moody Press, 1932), pp. 158–64.
3. Ibid.
4. Ibid.
5. Ibid.
6. Ibid.